To Aan

A TRUE SON IN

THE LORD, A WISH FOR

YOU THAT THESE WORDS

WILL INSPIRE NEW IMAGINATION

AND AN ANCHORED LIFE IN

THE KINGDOM!

Ben

— Tom

Goldfish
Bowl

TOM and the Goldfish Bowl

Ben Pasley

CHURCHthink
series

Find this book online for free on many open source book platforms. Why? Because we want everyone to read it.

Find it online in every ebook format for digital readers at www.bookshooter.com—*helping independent authors publish ebooks*—Bookshooter!

This book was created via a partnership with www.TheEmpowermentHouse.com—*a coaching service for the creative who wants to be profitably independent.*

Published by Blue Renaissance Publishing
743 Gold Hill Place
Woodland Park, CO 80866

Cover Design: Kyle Steed
Edited By: Laurie Thornton, Crucial Book Consulting

Printed in the Unites States of America

ISBN: 978-0-9825434-1-2
Library of Congress Control Number: 2009911631

*Dedicated to the late Bob Terrel who planted the seed,
and to Doug Roberts who now waters.*

TABLE OF CONTENTS

FOREWORD BY JACK TAYLOR

I love allegory for several reasons. It is, as in this remarkable work, often couched in fiction.

Allegory approaches through the back door when the front door is shut and sometimes locked, and by dressing up controversial truth in acceptable garb allegory may find the reader open to areas of discussion that otherwise would be avoided. In allegory one may speak hard truths so disguised as to cause the observer to lay aside defensiveness and be open to truths heretofore refused. This is just such an allegory, and just such a book.

We are good at picking up a book, reading a few chapter headings, observing the brief biography of the author, looking at the names of the endorsers, seeking for a few theological buzzwords and making a decision to lay it down because it violates some "lightly held" religious tradition. EITHER THIS BOOK WILL DEFY SUCH AN EXERCISE OR BREAK IT UP IN THE MIDST OF THE PROCESS.

Allegory can be entirely fictional and lacking in purpose or it may revolve around a truth so mighty, so indispensable to our lives, so indescribable that it sends the reader on a life-altering saga. There is no doubt in my mind that *TOM and the Goldfish Bowl* is the latter.

Never has the Christian world been offered so much information on the Kingdom of God and, while it is welcome, it can be overwhelming if not confusing. This work will emerge, in my opinion, among the most clarifying offerings on the delicate discussion of the Church, the Kingdom of God and the traditions of men. To the open and searching heart it will encourage us to believe that it is all right to lighten up and, with tongue in cheek, have an honest and "ouchy" look at our funny, religious selves.

Ben Pasley is a binary genius (look it up), funny, loose and loaded with good sense. Is there such a word as *trinary* or *quadrinary*? If so, that too may describe Ben.

Thanks Ben, for a novel, pertinent, and a fetching trip into a field of truth that not only challenges our practice of faith, but also helps our sense of humor as we consider our sometimes laughable religious positions. You have moved us to be daring dreamers of approaching seasons when we will abandon sad and senseless traditions and take up the banners of praise and worship. Because you have helped us see him as he is, we can more excitedly worship, walk and serve him as we ought.

I feel somewhat guilty about having detained you from the excitement of what's ahead in this welcome and exciting work. But humor me, I've enjoyed looking it over. Now, for goodness sake get on with it!

Jack Taylor, President
Dimensions Ministries
Melbourne, Florida
November 10, 2009

PART ONE:

THE WATER, THE FISH, AND THE LITTLE HOUSE

Society for the Ethical Treatment of Goldfish

Henry stood, motionless, in front of the wall of fish choices. It was early in the morning—at least by his standards—and his ability to make a quick choice was stunted.

No coffee yet.

The fish tanks were stacked high and wide on the display wall, bubbling and humming and constantly moving.

They say this lowers your blood pressure, he thought.

He blurred his eyes at the wall to diminish all of the fish motion and he focused on the price tags alone.

Cheap is good; cheapest is best, he chanted to himself.

His eyes scanned the hypnotic wall to the left away from the crabs and saltwater fish, skipped over the bigger freshwater fishes and frogs, and was just settling on the seventy-nine cent price tags when—

"Can I help you?" The Walmart lady had snuck up on him, and when she spoke he jumped and found himself face to face with her.

"Uh, mmm, yeah, I need some of these goldfish," pointing at the tank on the lower left of the wall.

Her eyes bounced down to the goldfish bowl on the floor at Henry's feet. The goldfish bowl was a great deal. It came with all the goldfish accessories.

"How many you gonna put in there?"

"Maybe a dozen."

"That's too many for that bowl. They will die," she said with a more than obvious tone of disapproval. She continued to instruct him on how many goldfish could live for how long in certain sized bowls and made sure that all of her insights and her disapproval of his present direction were known to most of the pets, tools, and people in the greater sporting goods area. To him, she seemed to be strengthening her position for an intervention of sorts. It was funny-awkward and it caused him to smile in the corners of his mouth as he turned back to the wall of fishes. So many choices. Goldfish were definitely the cheapest and they were definitely the best choice.

When we are done today my boys can take care of them, Henry thought, and we can even relocate them if we need to in order to keep the water clean.

"I'll take twelve, please."

"You know they are not going to live."

"They will be fine."

"What are you going to do with them? Are they goin' in this bowl?"

Oh, yes, they were going in that bowl, and he knew it was going to be awesome. He also knew that trying to answer her question would be a mistake—not because there was anything unsavory about his purposes but because he knew that explaining the use of a goldfish bowl to create a living illustration of the relationship between the Kingdom of God, the Church, and the traditions of men was amusingly outside the scope of the present conversation. He exhaled a partial laugh out of his nose while thinking about how funny it would be to try.

"Thanks for helping me with this, but they will be fine."

Their was never really a confrontation because the Walmart lady had never looked directly at Henry, nor had he been looking directly at her. He had been glancing over the wall of fishes, his mind drifting in and out of the present moment beside the humming bubbling fish tanks to the rest of the day. She, on the other hand, had been retrieving a net and a plastic bag from the display area the whole time she was loud-talking.

She asked him something about the color of fish he preferred, which was of no concern to him, and with cooing love language she continued scooping and coaxing the fish into the net. Within a minute she had twisted off the top of the clear bag, slapped a price sticker on the side, and said, "They won't live long in that bowl."

"Thanks," he said, smiled, and picked up the rest of his stuff and turned toward the checkout area.

I wonder if they train them to do that or if that was purely personal.

There were no lines at the checkout stands.

The 70's Are Alive and Well

Jack and Lillian had picked their new rental home via the internet before they moved. It was a difficult process—as you could imagine—sorting through pictures on a computer screen, but their eyes and instincts had led them to the perfect place. It was a quaint little house on the top of a rise on the north side of town that could, in the winter, see through the taller trees and glimpse the outline of the Colorado fourteener, Pike's Peak. It was painted a pale gray-blue with a bungalow roof pitch, and a wrap-around deck on three sides that caught the southern sun. What they liked the most was that the interior was completely decorated and appointed with the colors and textures of the decade in which it was built—the Seventies! Complete with pebble-pattern linoleum, light pine paneling, and a white floating fireplace on the living room wall, this place had accidentally become trendy by simply never changing. It was the perfect place for Jack and Lillian to host parties, and, so, they volunteered their new home as a place to host the day retreat.

This day retreat was very special and one of the first of its kind. It was called a Churchthink retreat. Henry was the architect behind its design, but friends like Jack and Lillian had brought it to life. Most of their friends loved Jesus and were fully committed to living a life obedient to God and his dreams for their lives. This retreat was tailored just for them. They were beautiful people with a growing awareness of their unique destiny in God. Many of them were very talented artists, some were leaders at a local fellowship, and some self-identified as missionaries.

More important than being artists, pastors, or specialists in a spiritual work, the retreat guests were first, people. They were people who believed in God, and they were people who had been searching to understand the longing in their hearts. That longing was to understand not only God's dream for their personal lives, but also God's dream for how they fit into the bigger picture. It was this longing that motivated Henry to invite them to the retreat. It is easy to notice in anyone's journey the questions they might pose about "God and me," but Henry had made note of these friends whose questions had begun to include "God and us." This transition in thinking requires more attention, and it requires more conversation about bigger themes like community, Church, family, and the Kingdom of God. The Churchthink retreat was one way to establish value for these "us" questions and to set aside special time for finding some answers.

By nine o'clock on Friday morning people had begun to arrive. Taking off their coats and shoes at the entry to avoid bringing the snow onto the linoleum, most were taking turns introducing themselves, exchanging hugs, giving directions to the coffee carafe, and claiming a seat in the spacious living room. The coffee table was not moved, but the couches and chairs around it were opened up and additional seating was brought in to make room for the twenty or so guests who would enjoy the day together. It was a haphazard circle of seating that was open at the fireplace and broken in one place to allow access to the front door. In the other direction were the coffee and snacks.

"Which one is decaf?" someone asked, looking at the two tall coffee carafes.

Several people mocked the idea of decaf.

Misha, a consummate outdoors-woman, talked about her plans for an all-girl hike into the mountains the following week. Two guys were fighting over a chair with a footrest. Henry piddled around the coffee table.

It didn't take long for scattered morning conversations to settle and for everyone in the group to claim a place for themselves and a corner of an end table for their coffee cups.

The Bowl of Water

Henry leaned toward the coffee table (from where he sat he could touch it), and invited the room to turn their attention toward three items that were placed on it. In the very middle was a goldfish bowl. This bowl was flat on the bottom so it could stand on its own and its top was perfectly round and open to the air. It started out as a globe, of course, but in order to provide a better viewing area, it was flattened out on two sides —sort of like an apple that has had a quarter knifed cleanly off opposing sides—providing a clear window into the world of the fishes. The goldfish bowl was almost full of water.

"The first item I would like you to focus on is the goldfish bowl. It is our first element. Now, each of these elements represents something spiritual. I want you to consider the nature of these things, words that come to your mind, descriptives, et cetera, as we go along."

By this time everyone was settling into their places, and the morning hubbub was dying down.

"As you consider the goldfish bowl, I want you to include the water as part of the element." He made quotes in the air when he said *element*. "This way, when we refer to the goldfish bowl we are thinking about the water and the bowl together as a place. It is an atmosphere, a place to live."

"If you are fish," quipped someone.

The Tiny House

Henry picked up the next element, admired it, and laughed aloud as he began to describe it: "Yesterday, when I was pulling the elements together I realized I needed a small house, but I didn't know the exact size I needed and I didn't think I could just find one to buy, so ... this is the work of my eight year-old son." There was some laughter and commentary about the creative license that had been taken in interpreting the shape and design of a "house" and someone offered a comment on the nice roofline. Henry continued as he rotated the little house, "I said, 'Eno, go get your Lego bricks and build me a little house that is about this size, and I want it to have huge windows and doors so you can see all the way through it from any angle.'"

The little house was tall with large openings placed in odd rhythm around all four sides. It had very steep Gothic roof lines and all the roof bricks were black. The rest of the house, however, was put together with a more-is-more color value system as every Lego color was well represented.

Henry put the little house back down on the coffee table and underlined that it was the second of the two elements to consider.

The Goldfish

"Here is the last element for our word picture," he said as he lifted a small plastic bag filled with water and about twelve bright orange goldfish. While telling a bit of the story of the fish-Nazi at Walmart, Henry held the bag up high in the light and encouraged everyone to focus not on the bag or the water, but only on the fish themselves. He enjoyed the diversion of the story of purchasing the fish, and it allowed the room to enjoy the real-time nature of the conversation.

"Are you going to eat them?" someone squirmed.

"No, because the fish-Nazi will hunt me down!"

Everyone made appropriate noises and gestures based on their own reaction to the idea of eating a goldfish. Some were frighteningly excited about the prospect, and others made terrible faces. Henry, exploiting the moment, shared a useless insight on how to put pieces of carrots shaped like goldfish into the bowl to trick junior high kids into thinking that you were eating a real one. He mimicked wiggling the imaginary carrot between his fingers before popping into his mouth and crunching it up, mouth open! Again, there was a mixed response.

As the room slowly settled down he recovered his serious face and began to speak about the elements. While pointing at each he said, "So, on the table are three elements: the water, the little house, and the goldfish." Everyone focused a bit more, and then with a bit of a wink behind his smile he asked, "Which one represents the *Kingdom of God*? Which one represents *the Church*? And which one represents the *traditions of men*?"

He enjoyed that quiet moment ... for just a moment. It was a short space. The energy level notched up several degrees and the answers and ideas started to flowing around the room. There were a few debates on small points, but in just a few minutes the group had decided what each of the three elements represented.

The Atmosphere of the Kingdom

Henry leaned back in his chair and enjoyed the spiritual discernment that was taking shape. He encouraged them that they were all on the right track, and then said, "Let's consider the bowl of water first, and how it represents the Kingdom of God.

"Remember, when Jesus speaks of the Kingdom He goes in two directions that are easy to remember. One is that he describes it *as a way*. He might say, 'The Kingdom of God is like...' and he would go on to tell a story of a farmer sowing seed, a merchant looking for pearls, yeast being worked into bread, a king preparing a wedding banquet, or a landowner hiring workers late in the day. All of these things describe what the Kingdom is like when we can see it with our eyes. I think Jesus used word pictures so that we could find real life examples of how the Kingdom really works. This, of course, implies that the Kingdom does create real, measurable results in our present world. Well, why wouldn't it? We don't believe that Jesus will only have ruling influence in the future do we?"

Henry let this last question float out over the room just for a moment to see if there would be any wrestling with that idea; then he went on.

"The other direction that Jesus takes in relationship to the Kingdom is in *promoting its location*. He often makes a point to declare that it is near. He also makes notes about entering it or where it is around us. This is important because He was not exclusively describing a Kingdom that we would one day arrive at, but he was proclaiming a Kingdom that exists, in some way, in this present world. The Kingdom seemed to be waiting for people to realize it existed. By *realized* I mean acknowledged, maybe welcomed, or agreed with. He wants us to wake up to it.

"In Luke 10, he tells the disciples to 'heal the sick who are there and tell them, "The Kingdom of God is near you."' It was as if to say that when the Kingdom exists, and when it is has partners on the earth that agree with it, then people get healed. The disciples were instructed to confidently believe that the Kingdom was near us—all around us—and that it was *the unique atmosphere of the purposes of God*."

"Whoa ... say that again," Matt said, as he fumbled for his pen and paper.

"The Kingdom of God is the unique atmosphere of the purposes of God."

Henry stopped and studied the faces of his friends to see who was tracking and who was struggling with the connection he had just made between the goldfish bowl and the Kingdom of God.

"Questions?"

Matt, who had now assembled his pen and paper, said, "You are saying the the goldfish bowl represents the Kingdom of God because it is like an atmosphere—like an ecosphere for the purposes of God?"

"Yes, and I like that you used the word *ecosphere*. That has a great application for this moment. The ecosphere was introduced as a little glass globe—totally sealed—that had some water and air, some little plants and a few tiny shrimp in it. Its claim to fame is that, even when totally sealed, the plants and shrimp could survive for years without the glass ever being opened. I only bring it up because it is an experiment with creating a life-sustaining environment. An ecosphere is an environment where things can live temporarily, but I propose that the Kingdom of God is the environment that the family of God can live in forever."

"Whoa."

"Mmmm."

"Hmm?"

Thought-noises were emanating from around the room.

"Well, if the Kingdom is more like a place that we can live in," Matt asked, while pointing at the goldfish bowl, "then how do we see it as an action? Jesus often described what it was like in terms of action, so how does the atmospheric idea—which seems static to me—relate to the idea that the Kingdom is an action?"

Fish Need Water

There could not have been a more perfect segue, thought Henry as he stood and lifted the bag of goldfish. "Who did we propose these guys are?"

"The Church."

"Yes, that must be true. So let's put them where they belong." He carefully untied the top of the bag while supporting it with one hand under the bottom, and gently began to pour the fish and the water into the goldfish bowl. One, two, three, four, twelve ... all of them made it in and began to swim happily around the bowl of fresh water.

It only took a moment for a few folks to make the protracted "ah" sound as their light bulbs went on, and then answers came from all over the room:

"So the Church lives inside of the Kingdom."

"So the Kingdom is our atmosphere."

"The fish need the water to live and move around ... so..."

"Yes," said Henry as he moved back into his chair, "the fish need the water in order to really be themselves."

After a beat, he continued, "I mean, could a fish really be comfortable with its fish-ness if it were just laying on the coffee table? Could humans really act like humans and be natural if they were submerged in the ocean with no access to air?

"No, of course not. Living things need the appropriate environment in order to thrive. They need the system of life and breath and sustenance that feeds who they really are. The little brine shrimp in the original ecosphere could survive in that environment for a while. These goldfish will survive in this bowl for a little while. The question is: what do we need to really survive—or even better—what do we need to really thrive?"

Now Henry leaned over with one elbow on the arm of his chair and changed his tone, "I am going to pause for just a moment in our discovery of this allegory to underline this point about *being ourselves*. You know that I am talking about sonship. Sonship is how we enter into our new life with Father God. We were lost like homeless orphans until Jesus came and offered us a pathway to be reunited with our Dad. At the moment we believe in Jesus we are miraculously adopted into the family of God where Christ becomes our brother, God is restored to Fatherhood, and we become sons. Now, I believe with all my heart, that the Holy Spirit has come to help us understand how to be ourselves—our new selves—and that we are to have joy and adventure discovering what it means to live according to our new, true nature as sons. And now the passage in Matthew 13 comes to life for us when Jesus says, 'Then the righteous will shine like the sun in the Kingdom of their Father.'"

Still leaning on the arm of the chair, Henry scanned each face in the room and asked a few times: "Are you a son?"

The room responded with positive nods and noises. Henry pointed to the aquarium and continued, "In our allegory the fish's true nature is fish-ship."

His wife protested the word usage.

"Ok, fish-ship was hard to say, and a little awkward ... I won't say it again. The point is this: the best this fish can do is to be a fish. The best it can do is to be itself."

He moved closer to the bowl and pointed at one of the larger goldfish that had been swimming closer to the surface: "And, as it relates to the fishbowl and the water, this fish needs to be comfortable in and recognize the joy of its perfect environment in order to live and to thrive in its true fish-nature." He winked at his wife.

"OK, now," Henry centered himself on the front edge of his seat, and with obvious excitement he went on: "this is where it gets good. Ready?

"This is where we tie together the *atmosphere* of the Kingdom and the *actions* of the Kingdom. As sons who carry their Father's DNA, we must be ourselves! This really is our maturity. As sons we can become like our Dad because his Spirit is in us. Remember from 2 Corinthians 5, 'if anyone is in Christ, he is a new creation; the old has gone, the new has come!' Tell me, though, how can we become mature if we don't live in our perfect environment? Just as goldfish need water and food and oxygen, we are spiritual beings who need the right environment. Our environment—the ecosystem that supports our very way of life—is the atmosphere of the Kingdom of God!"

Turning toward Matt, he said, "To say it in a way that will address your question about how we see the actions of the Kingdom in the element of the goldfish bowl, I say it is in watching the fish be themselves!"

"Aaaagh," was the sound that Misha made while she was trying to make a sentence. Several other people imitated the part gagging, part epiphany-getting sound, and then she got out, "OK, I think I am getting it. What I am seeing is that the Church is all the fish..."

People affirmed with noises and nods.

"The fish are individually sons in the Kingdom, which makes them more of a family..."

More affirming notes were coming from the room.

"So we are sons who have our Father's nature, but we need the atmosphere of the Kingdom to help us act it out!"

Loud agreements followed.

Henry nodded, "True fish-nature is activated in the fish as they agree with the Kingdom all around them."

Fish Versus Water

Jack spoke up and affirmed Misha in grabbing the basics of the idea as he saw them and then went on to ask, "I have got to know more. What are we actually saying about the relationship between the Kingdom and the Church? I think we are saying they are not the same, but they are inseparable—at least in the goldfish bowl they can't be separated. At least that is what I am seeing. I mean, I realize that the Kingdom could be represented in a much, much bigger bowl than the one on our coffee table."

Henry interrupted to agree and encouraged everyone to imagine the Kingdom atmosphere to be as big as the whole world and more.

Jack went on, "A lot of people get really frustrated because they don't understand why the Church itself is not the Kingdom. It seems to be shocking to them. The idea that there is something more is really threatening to them, and the idea that the Kingdom might go out into places they do not go themselves also seems awkward. I actually feel like when I share just the idea of the power of the Kingdom with some people, they feel diminished and attacked by it rather than inspired. What is that?"

Rachel, who had been rather quiet up until then was already wrestling with the same issue began to share: "I think this picture is really beautiful. I have been staring at the fish—which is very relaxing—and thinking about how the fish don't fight the water. The water doesn't rage against the fish. They live in harmony and they are in no way threatened by each other, the very thought of that is kind of silly."

She turned to Jack, "Jack, I am not saying that your question is silly at all. What I am saying is that people who really struggle with the relationship between the Church and the

Kingdom are not looking at the same picture that we are looking at right now. They must have something else in their heads."

"I think you have hit it head-on, Rachel," Henry said in stride. "You guys are both touching on something extremely important. It is very true that people have ideas in their heads about the Church itself that makes these ideas very difficult to absorb. We have all struggled at times with what words like *Church* really mean. The meanings of words stem from our beliefs and imaginations about ourselves, God, and who we are together. I can explain it better as we continue on in our discovery of this word picture, but we could stop and make this footnote in our hearts: if we imagine the Church as an institutional fortress where we rule our doctrinal territory, then whatever seems to be outside its protective wall will be automatically viewed as the enemy. This imagination tells us that either the Kingdom has to be contained within the walls of our system or we are missing something. You see, the tension Jack has discerned is not a problem with understanding the word *Kingdom*. It is a problem with the person's understanding of the word *Church* and what it really identifies. They really are, just like Rachel said, looking at a whole different picture in their heads."

Wanting to keep the crew focused on the allegory and not diverted into more complicated head spaces, Henry refocused on the coffee table and said, "This is a perfect time for us to introduce the third element into our allegory."

Henry lifted the little Lego house and asked, "What did we say this represents?"

TOM

"The house represents the traditions of men, I guess, because it is something made by men?" said Misha with an upturned question mark right at the end.

"There are several passages in the Gospel of Mark, but probably this one is the one most quoted," Henry continued as he thumbed through his Bible. "Mark, chapter 7 and verse 8 says, 'You have let go of the commands of God and are holding on to the traditions of men.' Now, here is where we have to draw a sharp distinction between the Church as Jesus would have us see it and the traditions of men as he speaks of it here. Look at the goldfish bowl and say it after me: 'The people are the Church.'"

Everyone said it: "The people are the Church."

"The little house is something man-made and it will never be the Church."

Everyone chimed in: "The little house is something man-made and it will never be the Church."

"Now, if we can just absorb the depth of that truth it will fix so many of our mental problems and our terrible misuse of language around these two basic truths. We have gotten into tons of trouble simply because we couldn't keep these two ideas separate. Now that we know the Church is always, and only, *the people,* let's go on and define what the traditions of men really are.

"People have often thought of tradition as something bad, especially young pioneers." Henry purposely made eye contact with a couple of folks to make room for questions or comments.

"But to think of tradition as equivalent to evil just can't be right. Look, Jesus was speaking to Jewish religious people who had really set a high mark on the number of rituals, washings, readings, and ceremonies that a person would be required to perform in order to try and do the right things. Today, we have continued that effort of creating the 'best,'" Henry made quotes in the air, "methods by adding dress codes, meetings, doctrines, politics, and manuals to instruct in almost everything in the culture of Christianity. Since we have it in our heads, however, that the passage in Mark is judging some traditions as evil in themselves, then the question has always been: 'Which one of our traditions is better than the other ones?' or 'Which of our traditions is evil?' Well, these questions are flawed to begin with, so both the questions and the answers, of course, have only bred more prejudice and more rhetoric that we use to push others' traditions down while holding ours up.

"Here is why the questions are flawed: Jesus didn't accuse the Pharisees of having bad traditions."

Henry let this last comment trail off so everyone could gather their thoughts. After a moment he said, "Let's do this: take out a piece of paper and a pen and write down five traditions of men that you feel you can identify in your own journey. I'm going to warm up my coffee while you are at it."

After pouring a short cup of very strong Joe he moved back to his chair, stretched a bit, and sat down. Just before everyone had completely finished he started taking responses. By the time everyone had shared, the list was long and contained a little bit of everything: traditions of baptism, worship styles, dress codes, missional doctrines, buildings, tithing, Charismatic stuff, Catholic stuff, big meetings, small meetings, leadership structures, denominations, and quiet times ... just to name a few. Then Henry asked, "Would you guys glance back at the verse, Mark 7:8, and tell me again what Jesus was actually criticizing them for?"

The responses came quickly.

"That's right," Henry affirmed, "the problem wasn't the tradition—at least that is not what he pointed out—it was that the folks had *let go of God's heart* and exchanged it for *holding on to* their traditions.

"Now that changes everything doesn't it?

"It is a matter of trust, love and devotion. It is a matter of priorities. I am not going to assert that any one thing that you listed on our very long list of the traditions of men are either good or bad at this point. I think that is the wrong road and we must avoid going down it. I want to talk about what position your traditions have in your heart."

Henry took the little house and began to press it carefully down into the goldfish bowl. One of the group warned of overflow, but Henry claimed with some drama that displacement volume had been carefully calculated. Just before the water pushed over the lip of the bowl, the house was completely immersed. The problem was, however, that there was too much air trapped in the walls of the tiny house and it wanted to float like a ship. "That will never do," noted Henry, and everyone set about a solution to get the house to sit upright on the gravelly bottom. Eventually, after a few solutions were proposed, someone came inside with a rock about as big as a fist and, with no sense of gracefulness, set it right on top of the house, mashing it right to the bottom of the bowl.

"Well, that's uglier than I had imagined," said Henry, as he reviewed the present rock-on-top-of-house visual, "but I guess you get the picture."

Someone quipped about it being a house in Pompeii.

"TOM!" barked Lillian from the back of the circle.

"Tom who?"

"Yeah, TOM," she said with absolute delight at her own wit, "Traditions of men." She spelled it out: "T. O. M. TOM. Let's call him TOM!"

After a good bit of laughter and colorful commentary it was quickly agreed that saying "The traditions of men" took too much energy, and so, TOM was adopted as a hip and needed acronym.

"Well, we are all tired of serving TOM," someone piped up. Several agreed.

"Yeah, we need to do something about TOM as soon as we can. He is pushy and bossy, and isn't relevant any more." The collective affirmed that one, too.

"Why do we need him at all?" asked another.

"Wait, now, all traditions can't be bad. Henry already said that," said Misha, who was visibly frustrated by the direction the group had taken in their attacks on TOM.

"Good point, Misha," Henry said hoping to change the focus on the conversation, "look at the fish." The fish were now moving around the new structure in their environment and poking around the edges of the house. "Do the fish like the new house, or have they been mortally threatened by it?"

The group began to murmur on that point, and rather than offer any direct answer someone pointed out, "Hey, that little one right there is going inside ... nope, he's out ... back in." As the fish became accustomed to the colorful house they more frequently darted in and out of it, and some seemed to like tucking in close to one side or near the wide doorways. Noticing the fluidity of the fish's behavior around the house, Henry asked again, "Do they like the house?"

"Yes, some do," came the concession.

"Does it threaten or help them?"

"Seems like some of them like it. It probably feels safe."

"What about the others?"

"Well, some go in and out without seeming to care, and there are a few who have not gone near it yet."

Henry says, "It seems a lot like the relationship between the Church and TOM as we actually know it. You see, some of you already wanted to revert to criticizing tradition as if it were intrinsically bad. You have to repent for that knee-jerk reaction and take on the mind of Christ, who made it very clear to the Pharisees, at least, that it was not the tradition he was concerned about ... it was that they were allowing their hearts to trust in it."

Fish-Freedom

Henry went on to explain, "What I mean is that we have affirmed that the Church *is* the living fishes in our allegory. They live and breathe and move about just being themselves. Individually we can see they are sons, or saints, or believers, and when we see them as a group we call them the Church. Now, we don't call the little building the Church because we know that is foolishness. But c'mon, how many of you as soon as we placed that little building in there wanted to see the little fishes 'go to Church?'"

After a confession or two and some light harassment around the room, Henry continued in a comforting tone, "Jesus didn't die on the cross to win himself some buildings or organizations. He died for people—that's where his heart is. Say it out loud, 'I am his people.'"

The room responded: "I am his people."

"Isn't it good to know you are at the center of his heart? Say, 'I am the Church.'"

They responded again: "I am the Church."

"Now, are you the Church whether you are inside that little building or not?"

The group harmonized, "Yes."

"Oh. Really?

"What about when you are around the edges of the bowl or in groups of two? What about when you won't come out of the building for fear of doctrine sharks? Are you still the Church?"

There were plenty of quick responses and some enjoyment of the idea of a "doctrine shark," but Henry took some time, made some follow-up notes, and engaged a few more questions that underlined the ideas of location: how the Kingdom was everywhere—limitless—but the Church was not limitless. She was limited by the location and the number of the people of God. The Kingdom, he said, was endless and vast, and it couldn't be contained by one structure or doctrine. It could not be limited by buildings or traditions. He finished by saying, "Well, neither can the Church be contained by one structure or doctrine, nor can it be limited by buildings or traditions."

The group drew obvious conclusions as the "water" of the Kingdom permeated the atmosphere, both inside and outside the little building they had named TOM. Someone made a particular note about how the fish seemed to have no trouble moving in and out of TOM and all around the bowl without any fear or sense of restriction. They had absolute freedom to be themselves anywhere inside of the Kingdom. This had particular resonance with much of the room, as many of the participants traveled and worked in all kinds of fellowships, missions organizations, and movements of one kind or another as worship leaders, teachers, equippers, and more, etc.

Henry landed a punch line right here in the conversation: "If you hold on to your traditions you will begin to confuse the Church—which is always and only the people of God—with the traditions she creates. If you hold on to something, you treasure it. If you treasure things that men have made, then you worship idols. If you treasure any tradition more than God's people, then you will have created an idol out of your tradition and God will not allow it to stand."

That took just a moment to settle into the room.

"Now let's talk about the struggle it is for people to receive the message of this goldfish bowl allegory when they have been told throughout their whole spiritual journeys that God only works inside of TOM."

A long, careful pause stilled the room.

He had a feeling that several needed to unwind this point a bit.

Misha was the first, and she spoke with some emotion in her voice: "You know, I feel that God is really speaking to me right now ... and it's mostly about me. I just realized that I have had an idea in my heart for years that kept me from feeling okay if I was swimming in the bowl but outside of the building— outside of TOM. I mean, I knew that I was still his, but whenever I would try to imagine playing music or doing anything outside of a traditional fellowship it just felt wrong." Misha was an incredible, veteran worship leader and traveling musician. "I have spent so much time trying to always prove that I was committed to being inside of a recognized tradition, or fellowship, or movement, or anything that would make me feel that I really belonged, that I never realized that I was the

Church no matter where I was! I just think God is really dealing with my heart right now. I think I am finally starting to see the Church as the people of God no matter what place they do or don't meet in ... and that really changes things. Wow, this might really free me up to do some things I have always wanted to do that never quite belonged inside of just one tradition. What this means to me—as far as the Church goes—is: *I always still belong.*"

"Incredible," said Henry, and the room agreed. "I think we can say, comfortably now, that TOM and the Church do not become synonymous—*ever*—and we should work to *never, ever confuse the two again.*"

TOM Gets a Promotion

"I am so excited about our perspectives getting changed so we can really see and celebrate the Church that Jesus loves," said Henry as he leaned back and put his hands behind his head. "This is such an important key to understanding who we are so we can be free to act like who we really are. Now, some believers are not free to be themselves because they have become trapped in inferior beliefs and low imaginations. They have never been outside of TOM, and they still confuse TOM with the Church. Remember when Jack was asking why some people seem to be offended when the Kingdom is talked about? I am going to give a broad answer to that exact question by asking you a question: What would happen in your mind if you were taught as a young fish that you could never leave the little house and be safe outside of it in the big waters? What if no one ever said anything about the bigger waters being scary, but you were simply taught that staying inside the little building was really *being the Church?*

"Well, this is much of what Misha was sharing from her journey."

Misha nodded. Some commented about fear. Others noted denominations, and others described doctrinal confinements. Eventually, someone offered the idea that confinement in TOM creates a sort of internalized prejudice, a sort of TOM-bigotry that lifts any need to reach out and connect, build unity, or enjoy any freedom in the greater family.

Henry said, "I propose that this is exactly where most of us have come from, and what most of us are still dealing with.

"You see, most of us met Jesus and were ushered into a group of some kind with a style, a teaching set, and a viewpoint of the world. Even if they didn't promote the walls of their tradition at all, we quickly constructed them on our own because it is our human nature to build homes, towns, and fortresses for safety. We build things we can belong to.

"However, something happens to us when we become sons of God by adoption. A new spirit is put in us that finds its true home in relationship with Father God and no longer needs wood and stone to give its heart a home. This new spirit is crying out, "Abba, Father," and is looking for a reality that meets its dreams of belonging to God's family in a huge and beautiful way. This always involves a deep desire to connect with one another in a meaningful, lasting way. Some are able to catch that beauty in their connections with other "fishes" and embrace their new family deep and wide, but some have, unfortunately, had their vision cut off by the walls of their tradition."

Henry took a sip of coffee to let that sink in.

"Notice that I didn't say their tradition was necessarily bad, but that having their vision cut off from the rest of the family is most definitely bad. I guess you could say that boarding the fish up in our little house right where it is would demonstrate that idea, but I want to show you another way a tradition itself really can become a dangerous force."

Henry moved forward, put his hand into the top of the bowl, and removed the rock that was holding TOM down. Then he pulled the house up so that it floated right on top of the surface of the water.

"Now, tell me, how long can the fish live in TOM in its present location?"

Henry grabbed the net and, against loud protest from several in the room, scooped up one unsuspecting goldfish and gently placed it in the house. Henry held on a bit and asked again, "How long will it live and be able to enjoy being itself inside of the traditions of men but totally out of the atmosphere of the Kingdom?" He held the little house just above the water level as the little fish flopped around a bit longer than was warranted. Then he put the fish back into the goldfish bowl where it swam on its way.

After sitting back down, he continued, "The way you felt when you saw the helpless goldfish is the way Dad feels when we get trapped in TOM's plans that have cut us off from the Kingdom and from our family. You know, in reality, I am not sure if we could ever really be in a place that had 'no Kingdom,' but I have certainly seen cases where TOM was promoted to such a great height that it seemed that all the Kingdom drained right out.

"Whenever TOM is promoted and elevated to a place so high in the minds of its leaders and adherents that they no longer recognize their love for the people of God and their need for the Kingdom of God, then the environment we need to live in starts to drain away. The sons might still be there, but they will wither and barely be alive.

"This promotion of TOM over all else comes in several packages. Sometimes it is by way of the self promotion of arrogant leaders who seek to preserve their tradition and their own high positions at all costs. Sometimes it is mutually accepted by spiritual slaves who are still working to be intellectually right for their salvation so they promote their *way* as *The Way* and they rule out the rest of the family of God all together. Sometimes it comes from blind, self-serving, unchanging prejudice that just wants to enjoy "our style" over all others and builds a wall of division between the people of God, which, of course, drains the Kingdom life right out of the system because Dad's heart can't support it. I like to remember this passage from Ephesians 4:

'Be completely humble and gentle; be patient, bearing with one another in love. Make every effort to keep the unity of the Spirit through the bond of peace. There is one body and one Spirit—just as you were called to one hope when you were called—one Lord, one faith, one baptism; one God and Father of all, who is over all and through all and in all.'"

After a short pause he concluded, "Jesus is not a polygamist."

TOM Finds His Place

"But I thought you said that all tradition wasn't bad?" someone asked from the kitchen.

"That is exactly right. Watch." Henry pushed the little Lego house back down to the bottom of the goldfish bowl and, as the fish began to swim around it and in it again, he said, "The only tradition that needs to be thrown out without further inquiry is one that won't let the fish love one another and be themselves. Boom. It's out."

The room took a moment to process.

On the end of the couch sat a tall blonde woman who had been content to write notes and remain quiet most of the day, but now she put down her pen and she drew a long breath before speaking. Calissa, sitting up to the edge of her seat, in tears, began to share her story: "I know exactly what that is like —to be held in a prison where you can't be yourself and where you can barely breathe or feel alive. I have struggled my whole life with just feeling like I was really important to God and had value as a daughter—or a son—like you have been saying. I was in a missions organization for years and years. It was a big deal, and we went on mission trips together, and I was really proud of being in it. Somewhere along the journey, however, the leader of my team pulled me aside and sat me down to bring some kind of correction to me for not obeying a rule of some kind. I don't remember the rule being a big deal, but what he said and how he treated me was a huge deal and it has haunted me for years. He attacked me with these stinging words: 'Just who do you think you are? Let me tell you something, you are no one unless I make you someone. And you are nothing until I say that you are something!'

'I have struggled with these words my whole life. I found out later he had said that to just about every girl in the group. I guess he just needed us to work for him."

Rachel, who was sitting directly across the circle, got up and moved over to where Calissa was sitting, tears began to flow again and a sense of careful slow-down filled the room. Rachel touched her shoulder and began to pray. She spoke with authority in her prayer that the curses spoken over her by this twisted leader would be broken off, and that she would be free to enjoy her daughterhood. There was lots of agreement, lots of words of affirmation toward Calissa, and many understood that she had suffered inside a tradition that was selfishly promoted and that most of the Kingdom had, indeed, been drained right out.

After a good while Henry spoke again and said, "Many people have grown up in a tradition where TOM speaks to them the same words: 'Just who do you think you are?' We can be free of that cursing question. We can live the joyful life of sons, but we have got to believe the truth about ourselves."

Fish-Faith

"You see," he went on, "Jesus said the truth would make us free. If we believe lies, we will be not be free. I mentioned earlier that some, especially those who are shocked by our allegory of the relationship between the Church and the Kingdom, have become trapped in inferior beliefs and low imaginations. Friends, it is not that they are not loved by God or that they aren't really sons, they just don't believe they are really sons, and therefore they don't have the power to live like it."

Henry grabbed his Bible off of the end table nearest him and fumbled for Luke 15. Holding up the Bible he asked, "What is the most popular parable in the whole New Testament?"

The parable of the prodigal son was the answer.

"I think you are right. Let's look at it together. I am going to propose that we give this parable a new title, however. Let's call it the parable of *Two Boys Who Didn't Know How Much Daddy Loved Them.*"

He quickly went over the basics of the story, beginning with the younger son who left home in order to spend his inheritance trying to find himself. Henry explained, "The younger son left home with all that his father had given him and spent it experimenting in pursuits of pleasure, as lost sons often do, and quickly started living as a slave. He tried to get menial work just to eat, but none of his work could restore his lost heart or fill his stomach. He woke up one day desiring to go home, but even as he went he was still identifying as a slave. On the long walk home he practices what he will say to his father: 'I am no longer worthy to be called your son; make me like one of your hired men.' You see, this boy left his father because he had not found himself a home in the love of his father, and as he returned he still did not know who he was. He believed he was a slave."

Henry was on the edge of his chair now.

"What saves us—what truly delivers us—is how Daddy God meets us when we come home. Even when we have the worst and most foolish ideas about ourselves he meets us on the road crying, 'Son!'"

Henry scanned the room slowly and repeated this proclamation of the father directly to several in the room:

"Son!

"Son!

"Son!

"No matter what you believe about yourself, when you come to back to God you find out that he only sees you as his son and he will refuse to treat you any other way. He will honor you with the robe of his approval, the ring of his authority, the sandals of trust to be his son anywhere you go."

With a wink, Henry said, "You did notice that the father put shoes on the feet of the son that was prone to wander didn't you?

"These shoes represent how much our heavenly Father trusts us to be ourselves wherever we go and how our place in his heart cannot ever change. And, finally, he rewards the younger son with more food and celebration than he would ever be able to consume at the party ... he gave him a whole cow!

"I bet at that moment the son remembered that in all his menial labor he remained hungry, but in the presence of his father—even before he had done a single thing of usefulness around the house—he had more than he would ever need."

Glancing back at the Bible he read, "'Meanwhile, the older son was in the field. When he came near the house, he heard music and dancing. So he called one of the servants and asked him what was going on.'

'This older son didn't know who he was in the eyes of his father either, but he had remained at home in order to keep doing what was right. Everyone in town knew that he had stayed while the younger brother had acted foolishly and left. I bet he gloried in that and derived some sense of identity from always doing the right thing and remaining close to the family business. But, he too, was just a slave in the field."

Henry continued reading, "'The older brother became angry and refused to go in. So his father went out and pleaded with him. But he answered his father, 'Look! All these years I've been slaving for you and never disobeyed your orders. Yet you never gave me even a young goat so I could celebrate with my friends.'

"This brother, though he looked like he had it together, was just as lost as the younger. He thought he was a slave as well. He thought he could work for his father's favor because he didn't know how much his dad loved him. He was so disconnected from his dad's heart that even if he were to get the goat he asked for he would have celebrated out in the corner of the field with his own friends, not with his dad.

"His dad says to him, 'Son, you are always with me, everything I have is yours.' You see, no matter what we believe about ourselves, our heavenly Father will always—because of Jesus—see us as his sons."

Henry leaned back and made sure he had the eyes of everyone in the room and said, "I want to remind you that in this challenge to grow in your sonship, I never said you were not sons. Tell me, were these two boys always sons?"

"Yes."

"Then the point of this parable is less about coming to God as a stranger and 'getting saved' and more about getting saved from not believing how much Daddy God loves you! Sonship is not built on the principle of obedience or the work of our hands. It is built on faith alone. We must believe and receive how much Father loves us or we will live just like the *Two Boys Who Didn't Know How Much Daddy Loved Them*."

Henry scanned the room with this eyes and asked, "Do you know that you are the Father's favorite son?"

Some affirmed it right away. Others hesitated.

Try saying it with me just to hear how good it sounds: "I am my Father's favorite son."

The group repeated it with some restraint.

"I am my Father's favorite son!" Henry said again.

This time, when the whole room said it, it felt bigger and deeper.

Swim!

Because he had made a commitment to the simplicity of the goldfish bowl allegory, Henry did not pursue any more related teaching points. It was, after all, just an allegory, and as such it would have its limitations and failures in addressing every aspect of understanding something as wide and wonderful as the nature of the Kingdom, the Church, and the traditions of men. His body was getting tired from being in the little leather chair all morning, and the smell of lunch—which was being prepared and set out on a buffet table while the talk was wrapping up—was more than anyone could stand.

He said in one last attempt to give the allegory legs for the rest of the day, "So, now that we are settling down into knowing who we really are we can begin to embrace the atmosphere of the Kingdom of God all around us. The Kingdom really is ours to enjoy—the healing, the forgiveness, the treasure hunting, and the responsibilities—because it all belongs to the sons!

"We don't need to take our assignments and run off or look for adventure elsewhere do we?

"No, because all the adventure and belonging we will ever need is in the loving eyes of our Father. Remember, again, Matthew 13:43, 'Then the righteous will shine like the sun in the Kingdom of their Father.'"

Someone asked, "So this is what being a fish is really all about?"

"Yes."

"So, let's all learn to swim!"

With that, someone was called on to pray a bit before breaking for lunch, and later the whole group enjoyed a long afternoon of more personal stories and insights around the fire in the outdoor pit.

PART TWO:

THE KINGDOM, THE CHURCH, AND THE TRADITIONS OF MEN

THE KINGDOM

I hope the first section of "Tom and the Goldfish Bowl" has been like a light flare over the fields of our collective imagination. Sometimes just a little light is enough to sponsor a "eureka" moment that can change us forever. Though I will not refer to the three-part allegory again in the remainder of this book, I do hope that it will continue to illuminate our thoughts as we go.

We Are More

What is the single most popular phrase that flows over the modern Christian's lips in an effort to connect with someone's spiritual journey for the first time? I think it is this: Do you go to Church?

I think the second most popular question would be: Would you like to go to Church with me?

Surely, we are more than meetings. Meetings are in many ways like handshakes. Handshakes are supposed to be the entry point into deeper relationships, but the world has grown tired of our culturally-relevant-rock-star-level-cause-driven-highly-orchestrated Church handshakes because there seems to be nothing beyond them except more meetings.

We are more than a first impression.

We have more than handshakes to give.

We are more than meetings.

The modern tragedy is that Christianity has been reduced to the action of going to meetings, and now *meetings* have become synonymous with our definition of *Church*. This invitation-to-meeting obsession has become a critical problem, and it has been pushing our reputations as followers of Jesus over the cliff of cultural irrelevance. We are becoming more aware all the time of how the obsolescence of Christianity is now a foregone conclusion in Western culture. Other words that now describe the Church's modern reputation might include *disconnected* and *out of touch*. Unfortunately, our lack of relevancy can't be blamed on Satan inhabiting the brains of movie stars and the so-called mainstream media. It is true that many have seen the Church as a broken, useless institution in recent years because of what some of its leaders have done to earn spots on tabloid television, but this broad judgement has become popular opinion for bigger reasons than the televised escapades of a few. I believe that we are, in many cases, being fairly judged. It seems that in many ways, especially in the ways that are most important to people in their spiritual pursuits, we have indeed become irrelevant. We have not offered much more than meetings, and the spiritually hungry have judged the offering as unacceptable. I believe this all stems back to one major mistake that we have all been making. I believe this one ongoing mistake has fueled our poor reputation and that it is the crisis at hand:

We have reversed the rightful positions of the *Kingdom of God* and the *Church*.

I will take the rest of the book to bring clarity to this crisis, and to bring clear solutions for our recovery. Dear Christian, we are supposed to be proclaiming the Kingdom and watching the Church grow as a natural byproduct, but instead, we have been proclaiming the Church hoping some Kingdom will come out of it. The proof of this backwards fixation is in how much we find ourselves preaching and proclaiming the Church. We just can't stop. We write books on how to make it better. We start movements of style and methodologies in order to revolutionize it. We promote the Church with all our might, and we do so fully believing that she is the answer for the world. That is fundamentally wrong, or Jesus would have gone about "proclaiming the Good News of the Church."

He did not.

We must repent.

We have continually upgraded our styles, our music, our language, and our websites because this, in our minds, has been the way to bring God-impact to our world. We have started Christian culture fist-fights over which established tradition or traditionless-tradition is better for the world.

We have missed the mark.

We have confused our priorities.

We have it upside down.

Jesus proclaimed the Kingdom of God and asked us to go and do the same: "When Jesus had called the Twelve together, he gave them power and authority to drive out all demons and to cure diseases, and he sent them out to preach the Kingdom of God and to heal the sick" (Luke 9:1-2), but we traded in this clear commission for what we thought we could see and understand better: the Church that meets together in buildings —large or small.

This trade has cost us dearly.

We cannot continue to work on perfecting our ideas of *Church* and how she should present herself, and expect the powerful, world-changing Kingdom of God just to pop out as a byproduct.

The Kingdom as Revolution

A *system*, defined, is simply the way that things work together. Now many believe, in keeping with their traditions, that in order to cure our present cultural irrelevance we should focus on fixing the present Church systems which obviously need improvement. Others think we should be punishing bad institutional Church systems and burning them all down because they are the true disease. Both of these directions are wrong because in both cases they attack the symptom but not the cause. The institutionalized Church, when it embraces marketing, management and intellectual territorialism is just exhibiting a symptom of a much deeper problem. It is a problem that runs deeper than systemic imperfection. I propose that all of these systemic sicknesses proceed out of this one root cause: *our failure to receive and proclaim the Kingdom of God.*

I am not sure how many people understand this failure because of the amount of effort we spend trying to build a better system and then we call it the *Church*. Our obsession with repairing the Church system is like an engineer's obsession to build a better mousetrap. The question arises, however, and we must pause to ask it: Why build a better mousetrap if catching mice is not even our responsibility?

Dear reader, why should we continue to obsess over building a better Church system if Jesus never asked us to do it in the first place? Why should we obsess over revolutionizing the structures of organizations if they have never been—and will never actually *be*—the Church? Has that ever been what God required of us?

I don't think so.

Jesus said, specifically, "*I* will build my Church." He never said, "Believers. Go and build the Church." So why have we spent so much of our time criticizing one system and proclaiming another if Jesus had already said that he *alone* would build it? Where did we get the idea that his Church is something that we could engineer? By counting the number of denominations and divisions in the Church today we have certainly proven our inadequacy in this regard.

I think it is worth the time to stop and emphasize that when Jesus spoke of the Church he was never imagining structures and systems at all. He did not call the *system* the *Church*. The Church may *use* a system, but she is not one. We have become confused between understanding the difference between the Church as the people of God, and the Church as the institutions that she has built and now occupies. Jesus never confuses the two.

Even while reading this chapter many of you have questioned my use of the capital "C" *Church* as I have made reference to her systems and institutions. Well, there is only one Church and we always capitalize her name because she is always the uniquely identified Bride of Christ. The Church is the people of God. If she has obsessed over inferior things, hidden away in institutional fortresses, or promoted temporal things—whether we like them or not—we still have no choice but to refer to her respectfully as the Church. Jesus was speaking only of his beautiful people when he said, "my Church" and in this book we will learn to do the same. Jesus claimed his unique authority to build her, and we will learn to let him do his business.

The Church is his responsibility.

Our obsession with getting into Christ's business has not gone well. Our misuse of the word *Church* to refer to buildings instead of people is living proof of how inadequate we are to try and fill his shoes. If it is obvious that we are doing a terrible job, then why do we continue? What drives us to continue in such misguided efforts? There is only one answer: *we have failed to receive and proclaim the Kingdom of God.*

Broken men have built broken systems with broken tools; therefore, every new improvement on the way men work and live together is destined to unwind and decay over time. Every new structure built by the hands of men still has flaws. We started trusting Church traditions and they quickly became institutions. People, even the people who were desperate to heal and improve these institutions, have passed this confusing disease along from generation to generation like unsuspecting carriers. Men have tried to inoculate themselves by dreaming up newer, and more perfect systems to contain the Church, but they have all been susceptible to the same human disease: brokenness. Many have lost hope and just left their idea of Church all together. But there is a hope.

There is a vaccine for this disease and it is 100% successful:

"Seek first the Kingdom of God." (Matthew 6:33)

The Kingdom of God must return to its rightful place as our obsession, our proclamation, and our reputation. The Kingdom can't be reduced to a collection of human ideas or traditions because it comes down from Heaven and does not have its origin on this earth. Believers, we were meant for so much more than what can be built by the minds and hands of men.

The Kingdom of God is our answer.

The Kingdom of God is what the whole world has been longing for!

The Kingdom as Family

Of course, we don't believe that all systems are bad. That is simply not true. There are systems that work and systems that don't. There are systems that are appropriate to the task, and systems that are bound to implode when misapplied. It is a mature discipline to discern the differences in systems and understand their effectiveness in any given situation. Some systems are excellent. One is perfect. This one perfect system began in the Heavens. It preceded creation in the mind of God. It has transcended all earthly tools and measures. And this system has found its way into our world.

It is all around us.

We discover this perfect system in pre-history when we discover God as the Trinity. We see it imparted as a foundation for this world on the sixth day of creation. We see it lasting into eternity when we dream about the wedding supper of the Lamb. Born in eternity, this system is bound for eternity and will live on forever. It has worked since the beginning of creation, and it still works well in every culture and nation on this earth. Constantly creative, reproductive, life-giving, self-propagating— it is a heavenly system that is now reflected in the jewel of the creation: humanity. It is the DNA code of the Kingdom itself. It is the blueprint for the way things work in the Kingdom. We call it...

Family.

Pause for just a moment and enjoy the simplicity of this one word—how far it reaches, all that it infuses and all that it transcends. Nothing stirs the romance of the human heart more than family.

Many of us have experienced the painful possibilities of broken family and shrink back from this idea out of instinct. This automatic response, however, is proof, not a refutation, of the transcendent power of *family* because it is in the knowledge that something perfect is calling to us that we are most profoundly aware of the pain involved in our failure to attain it.

Here is the Good News of the Kingdom of God: we don't have to attain it. And we don't have to fail any longer in our desire to have it.

We can receive it.

An invitation to join the perfect family has already been made by God. He continues to invite us in right now. It is the gift of God and it cannot be bought or earned. The Scriptures tell us that coming into the family is a journey of trust. "For it is by grace you have been saved, through faith—and this not from yourselves, it is the gift of God—not by works, so that no one can boast" (Ephesians 2:8-9). It is by faith, not works, that we are born again into family. It is a God-miracle. No one should ever believe the lie that we can earn it. The Kingdom is for sons and that is why we have to be born again to enter it (John 3), and we have to be adopted through blood to have it proven to us (Ephesians 2).

Would you like to enter into the family of God right now? Repent from your prideful independence. Trust your life completely to Jesus and believe that God has adopted you into his family. Live the miracle of becoming a son in the heart of God!

Family is the system of God's own heart, and it is the blueprint for our future. It calls to us. This call to our hearts is the "mystery" that Paul speaks of in Ephesians. It is the mystery that only Christ himself is able to bring to life and to fulfillment within us. It is the beautiful call to *be family with God*, and this call can only be answered by the power of the favored Son of God calls us into himself and transports us into a relationship of favor with our heavenly Father.

Kingdom Expression

The very reason that we have failed to "build the better Church" is because the Church is not a machine that can ever be built by men. It is the natural byproduct of coming together with God as his beloved family.

Being the Church is like water being the ocean. It takes no effort; it simply is what it is. The newly adopted sons of God, just as easily, are the Church—we are what we are.

The mystery of God that we enjoy is the mystery of becoming one family with him. What we can do, since we can't build Jesus' Church for him, is to proclaim this new freedom, this new favor, and this new position that comes by entering the Kingdom family of God.

We are called to build up one another: "He died for us so that, whether we are awake or asleep, we may live together with him. Therefore encourage one another and build each other up, just as in fact you are doing" (1 Thessalonians 5:10-11). This is a profoundly different work than the building and promoting of a perfect, man-made system, or the assumption that we can oversee the building of the whole Church. We can, however, help each other mature as members of God's family.

The people of God—the Church—are a living expression of the Kingdom, and their health is based directly on how well they embrace the Kingdom of God. The Church's purpose is to receive and proclaim the Kingdom of God. The Kingdom of

God *is* the Good News—the Gospel—which is the power to become God's family through Christ alone (Matthew 4:23).

Family can only be built and matured in a family way. Fathers share their DNA with their sons. Families pass along values to one another through close, loving relational pressure. Likewise, the DNA code of God's family is transmitted first from the Father to Christ who told his disciples in John 14, "Anyone who has seen me has seen the Father." This is the gift from the Father to his Son. Miraculously, through Christ, it is also his gift to us, "Therefore, if anyone is in Christ, he is a new creation; the old has gone, the new has come" (2 Corinthians 5). Now, we have a commission to share our Kingdom DNA with one another through close, loving relational pressure. This expression of our Kingdom DNA one to another is what we call the life of the Church. Church, therefore, is not the product of managers, schools, or mission statements...

Wait.

I need to slow down.

Please forgive the speed of this download. I am excited. I need to slow down, step back, and give more time for us to enjoy discovering the Kingdom of God together.

Let's take our time.

First, let's lets put some firm handles on the Kingdom of God. To do this I want to divide the New Testament writings on the Kingdom into four acts—like they do in a play where the lights go down and the curtain draws between each one. We will imagine these scenes playing out in real life. This imagination tool will allow us to group certain times and similar messages together, making it much easier to follow the big ideas in each one. Our theater acts will occur in order, over time.

ACT ONE:
The Kingdom Announcement

The Message of John the Baptist

The curtain opens on Act One.

We see John the Baptist standing in the River Jordan. He is preaching. Johns' words echo from Matthew 3: "Repent, for the Kingdom of Heaven has come near."

John was a seer. He was a prophet not only because he prophesied of the coming Messiah and the Kingdom of God, but also because he had eyes to see the Messiah. He knew it when he saw him.

John urged the people to repent and believe in the heavenly Kingdom and to turn from dead works, self-righteousness, and sin. He baptized those who said *yes* to his call and joined with him in agreement. John the Baptist's culture, as it were, consisted of those who would *repent* from trusting in the religion of men for righteousness and would *receive* the Messiah. This Messiah, according to John, would usher in the Kingdom of God and he would baptize with fire.

John looks up from the waters in which he was standing, and who does he see walking down into the edges of the Jordan? Who was walking toward John with his hands out as if to say, "It's my turn."?

It is Jesus.

John knew this man was the One, but he was confused: "John tries to deter him, saying, "I need to be baptized by you, and do you come to me?" Surely Jesus was not coming to be purified through baptism because he needed no such cleansing, John must have thought.

Jesus answered John, "'Let it be so now; it is proper for us to do this to fulfill all righteousness.' Then John consented" (Matthew 3:15). If Jesus' baptism was not because he needed to be purified from sin, then it was because he was identifying with John and his message. Jesus and John were being tied together, and Jesus wanted it to be so. Jesus was not only *with* John, but he would fulfill the righteousness John had been proclaiming. Remember, Jesus said the purpose of his own baptism was to *fulfill all righteousness.*

This new righteousness was not based on the works of men because it would come down from Heaven as a miracle-work from God. Jesus was going to make right relationship with God a real possibility, and he was going to do it inside of the Kingdom of God. We learn later in Romans that "the Kingdom of God is not a matter of eating and drinking, but of righteousness, peace and joy in the Holy Spirit" (Romans 14:17). Righteousness is of the Kingdom.

When Jesus enters the waters to be baptized he lifts John's message—the message of the Kingdom of God and this new righteousness that comes with it—to the ultimate height.

The inventor of baptism had entered the waters of baptism.

The author of righteousness was fulfilling righteousness in plain view.

The King of the Kingdom had arrived, and he was inaugurating his Kingdom.

When Jesus goes under the water we can imagine the fireworks going off in the Heavens. They are brighter than the midday sun ... the fire of God is preparing itself with excitement to reveal the nature of the new Kingdom.

Jesus comes up out of the water and—

He saw Heaven being torn open—

Heaven was torn open making way for something to come down on the earth.

And the Spirit descending on him like a dove—

When the Spirit descends we are aware of the feeling of a heavenly promise like the promise to Noah and the promise of a new era after an outpouring.

And a voice came from Heaven—

We realize that the Father is breaking any previous silence, and every atom of this world strains with excitement to hear what he will say next. So intense is the anticipation that for one moment the whole earth is perfectly still.

It is perfectly quiet.

Then the Father speaks the word that changes everything, forever:

Son.

A Kingdom of Sons

Now we realize what the climax of the Kingdom's message will be. We can see exactly *how* this new right relationship with God is to be established. We heard it right at the beginning when the Father spoke his heart aloud: "You are my Son, whom I love; with him I am well pleased."

Now, we know the very nature of the Kingdom, and we see it in these three phrases:

- It is the Kingdom of a Father.

- It is a Kingdom given to a Son.

- It is a family Kingdom.

It is a Kingdom whose very nature and strength and identity will begin—and will continue—with the proclamation: *You are my son, and I am very pleased with you!*

The Father establishes the tone of the Kingdom by letting us know how he will see us when we choose to trust Jesus and follow him. He sees us as sons, and we can't change it. We are to submit to his great, adopting love!

The Father speaks over us with love and pours out his Holy Spirit on all of us. The heavens themselves are opened up around us, and there is no more distance between. The Kingdom has been ushered in and it has become our very atmosphere. It is the atmosphere in which the Father and all of his sons love and live together.

The Trap

Now we leave the river, and we are taken to the desert to witness this scene from Luke 4: "Jesus was then drawn away to the desert to be tempted by Satan for forty days."

The liar is going to ask Jesus in many ways and with slick words: Do you really live inside of God's absolute favor as his son?

In the first temptation the devil tempts Jesus to do a miracle and eat what this world can offer, but Jesus answers, "'It is written: 'Man does not live on bread alone, but on every word that comes from the mouth of God.'" In other words, Jesus expresses, "I don't crave anything else to make me feel complete. I can see my Father's love for me in his eyes." Jesus still has the booming words of his own Father's approval fresh in his memory, and the sweet communion with the Spirit of adoption still fresh in his heart. He is full of confidence.

In the second temptation, the devil tries to lure him to create a radical, supernatural deliverance from death in order to find fame. Jesus responds, "'It is also written: 'Do not put the Lord your God to the test.'" In this response we hear: I don't need to perform to be a son. I don't need to test God because I trust his heart is always for me. I am already famous in his eyes. Jesus had not forgotten the incredible endorsement of his own Father when Jesus came up out of the waters of baptism. People only *test* what they don't know to be true. He knew what was true and he easily overcame the devil.

In the last temptation: "Again, the devil took him to a very high mountain and showed him all the kingdoms of the world and their splendor. 'All this I will give you,' he said, 'if you will bow down and worship me.'" Jesus quickly answers this ridiculous temptation to claim a temporary throne offered by the liar: I love my Dad and I would never trade my relationship with him for this nonsense. I will worship God alone. Jesus was not shaken in the least. It is easy to anchor our lives in Father God when we believe what he has said about us is true.

We should not think that this temptation drama was a show of Jesus' struggle at a moment of mental weakness.

No.

His body may have been weak, but his mind was clear. Jesus set the example for all of us. He set the example for sons.

It pleased Jesus to show us how foolish our enemy's attempts to trap us really are. We can follow suit as God's sons and say to the liar as well: What, you want us to trade in our eternal destiny in God, our place in the eternal Kingdom family for this?

A piece of bread?

Fifteen minutes of fame?

A fleeting earthly throne?

Back off. I am a son!

When we think of it this way we can see that the devil didn't lure Jesus as much as Jesus lured the devil! Jesus lured him in and trapped him in his foolishness so we could all see how easy it is for sons to defeat the liar. We should consider renaming this temptation episode: *How To Make the Devil Look Stupid.*

Believers, it is time for us to follow Christ. This means we must receive the words of favor that our Father speaks over us: *You are my son, and with you I am very well pleased!*

We must also receive the blessing of the Holy Spirit who has been sent from God to convince us, daily, of our Father's great love for us.

We must also be sure that we have an eternal destiny in God —as sons—and there is no foolish trick of the devil that will ever overcome us.

We will not be overcome when the liar comes and asks us in many ways and with slick words: "Are you really a son?" We will have an answer.

—∞—

ACT TWO:
The Good News of the Kingdom

—∞—

The Arrival of the Kingdom

At the beginning of Act Two we see Jesus standing in front of a crowd.

He is saying to the people, "Repent, for the Kingdom of Heaven is near."

There are four accounts of Jesus' life, the New Testament books of Matthew, Mark, Luke, and John. We call them Gospels. Gospel means good news. The arrival of the Kingdom of God is the theme of all four of these books.

"The time has come," Jesus says in Mark 1:15. "The Kingdom of God is near. Repent and believe the good news!"

In Luke 4:43 Jesus says, "I must preach the good news of the Kingdom of God to the other towns also, because that is why I was sent."

The Kingdom, we see, *is* the Good News.

Many have said, no, the good news is salvation, the good news is healing, the good news is being born again. And we might agree with them all. These things are all good news. But they are also just the natural fruit of the Kingdom of God.

It is good news to be able to start our lives over in God. Our purpose, however, is not just to be born again. Our purpose is on the other side of being born again. Jesus clarifies the purpose of being *born again* to Nicodemus in John 3:3: "I tell you the truth, no one can see the Kingdom of God unless he is born again." That's right: to see the Kingdom of God is the *purpose* of being born again.

Many believers, it seems, want everyone to be born again so they can be forgiven of their sins and then go to meetings. This is not the purpose of the rebirth. Birth is something that happens naturally in family. Birth brings us into family. In Nicodemus' case, as well as in ours, if we are born again it means that we have entered into a new heavenly family.

We have been born to our heavenly Father.

We have become his sons.

The purpose of our rebirth is to enter the family Kingdom of God.

This message of the Kingdom family dominates all of Jesus' life and teachings in the Gospels. The amazing dominance of the Kingdom message permeates all of the life and words of Jesus; there are over 100 instances of the word *Kingdom* in the Gospels alone. Luke 16:16 declares the Kingdom of God has divided human history: "The Law and the Prophets were proclaimed until John. Since that time, the good news of the Kingdom of God is being preached, and everyone is forcing his way into it."

The message of the Kingdom is violent because it has turned the direction of all human history on its head. It has interrupted our slide down the steep slope of independence and isolation from God, and offered us what we never dreamed could be ours: *eternal family*.

The Kingdom is a Way

The sheer amount of Christ's teachings on the Kingdom means we can only summarize them in our short book. Though it is imperfect to do so, I believe it can be helpful to group his Kingdom teachings into two main categories: understanding the Kingdom as a *Way*, and understanding the Kingdom as a *Location*. For the sake of fluidity we will not stop and reference all the Scriptures here, but they are all available in the bibliography.

The following two passages are meant to creatively condense the salient teachings on the Kingdom from the New Testament, and then "unpack" those teachings into practical, real time challenges that we can respond to.

BIBLICAL INSIGHT: Jesus and the disciples preached the Gospel of the Kingdom constantly. Whenever they proclaimed it people were often healed of every disease and sickness. Jesus sent his disciples out into the world to proclaim the Kingdom and heal the sick. Later, people were baptized as they received the message and chose to follow Jesus. Preaching the Kingdom takes work and perseverance and it demands a response from those who hear it. (Matthew 4:23; Luke 9:2, 9:11; Acts 8:12)

OUR RESPONSE: We hear the message of the Kingdom. We hear Jesus inviting us into his family and making a way through his own blood. We receive the message, and we trust in Christ alone to reunite us with our heavenly Father. We are now ready go and proclaim the Kingdom as sons. We expect miracles and the healing of every kind of sickness wherever we proclaim the Kingdom of God. If it gets hard or if we suffer, then it will be to glorify God, as this is also our inheritance.

BIBLICAL INSIGHT: When people learn that the Kingdom is their inheritance, they draw closer to God. They stay in the Presence of God because their inheritance is to enjoy the privilege and nearness of the Father's love. This Kingdom inheritance establishes privileges, authority, and heavenly resources that are immediately available. The poor in spirit who are hungry for God and those who suffer for their belief in the Kingdom for Christ's sake are sure to inherit the Kingdom. The Kingdom will be given to those who produce spiritual fruit, and only those who come from the Father can really bear the fruit of the Father. The Kingdom belongs to the sons. Jesus says to his disciples with a sincerity that only comes from family connection, "Do not be afraid, little flock, for your Father has been pleased to give you the kingdom." (Matthew 5:3, 13:23; 25:34; Luke 12:32)

OUR RESPONSE: The Kingdom is our inheritance because we are sons. If we suffer because we are in Christ and share his name, then it proves we are family. We are not imposters because we do not live as slaves trying to please God, but we walk in his favor always as sons. It is our privilege to enjoy his favor just as the prodigal son returned home to find it was never removed, and as the older son in the same parable came to realize it was always around him. We have come home to our heavenly Father. We are going to walk in Father's favor, Father's provision, and Father's authority as we go. This is how we *live* in Christ.

BIBLICAL INSIGHT: Those who accept the invitation to come to the wedding celebration will get to join the party. Those who love the Bridegroom will enter an eternal relationship with him. Those who do evil, imposters with no heart for the Bridegroom, those who will not help the poor and the widows, and those who won't receive the message of the Kingdom will not inherit the Kingdom because they prove that *they are not family.* Regardless of outward benevolent activity, it will be those who receive their adoption as sons that prove they belong to God. (Matthew 13; Matthew 22:8; Matthew 25)

OUR RESPONSE: We love you, Jesus. We accept your invitation to an eternal romance and an eternal commitment. As your dearly beloved we are confident in your love for us, and we rest in the fact that our hearts are falling in love with what you love. Jesus, You love your people, and we love your people, too. We love the Church and we commit to serving her. We will reach out and love the poor and forgotten as well. The Kingdom of God is a party and we are going to celebrate!

BIBLICAL INSIGHT: The Kingdom can be sought like a treasure in a field or a pearl of great price, and it is pursued with great violence by those who decide they must live with God. It is worth every effort, no matter how great. It is very powerful and can transform its environment like yeast in bread. And though it is a simple truth to receive, it can grow enormously larger and stronger, like a mustard seed into a mustard tree. We commit to work the Kingdom leaven, the promise of family, into all that we do. It is our nature to spread family love because it changes everything it touches. (Matthew 11:11-12; Matthew 13)

OUR RESPONSE: We are willing to repent and sacrifice what we were holding on to and take hold of what Father has for us. We have been adopted into his family, and we will grow and reproduce loving family just as his Kingdom DNA code has established it. Our work may seem small, but it will grow large.

Our lives are important. This Kingdom growth cannot be stopped. We are riding on the powerful wave of our new nature in Christ!

BIBLICAL INSIGHT: It is a great responsibility to serve in the Kingdom so we focus on being fruitful by loving and serving people. The Kingdom requires us to forgive one another so we don't choke the power of the Kingdom. The Kingdom cannot and will not be hidden by men. It must be revealed and allowed to shine, or we prove that we have no idea what we have received. We will never withhold the invitation to Father's family. This is a reflection of our relationship to God. Humility is our nature. (Matthew 13, 18; Mark 4:21-23)

OUR RESPONSE: We love to forgive. We are reconcilers. Any unforgiveness brings division and broken relationship and harm to God's family. We help bring people together as his family, and we joyfully and without shame promote the family of God everywhere we go. We are a family of selfless lovers and Jesus is our clear example of how far we are called to selflessly love. Whenever we promote ourselves and our strength we diminish ourselves and the family, but whenever we give ourselves to others in love, we build the family of God and Jesus is lifted up. This is an operating principle of the Kingdom of God.

The Kingdom is a Location

BIBLICAL INSIGHT: There are requirements to enter the Kingdom; not just anyone can enter. To enter the Kingdom you have to be born again of water and Spirit, and you have to be more righteous than the Pharisees. To enter the Kingdom you have to do the will of the Father. The Kingdom is a spiritual place and we can't enter it with human efforts. (John 3:3; Matthew 5:20, 7:21)

OUR RESPONSE: We realize that Jesus is the key to entering the Kingdom. Jesus is the complete answer to all of the entrance requirements of the Kingdom. When we live in him we live inside of his righteousness, which exponentially exceeds that of the Pharisees. When we walk in him we do, indeed, walk in his Father's favor and are walking in the middle of the Father's will. We can never earn for ourselves what our great Father in Heaven has given to us as a gift: the gift of adoption, which explodes in us by the Holy Spirit!

BIBLICAL INSIGHT: Getting into the Kingdom can be very hard. Jesus said some had to *force* their way into it. Some may have to painfully remove obstacles and endure hardships to get in. The rich and the prideful religious are going to have a difficult time getting in. However, those with the faith and humility of a child will have no trouble at all. Trust is the key; everyone must repent in order to enter. (Luke 16:16; Mark 9:47, 10:24-25; Acts 14:22)

OUR RESPONSE: We realize that human effort will not help us enter the Kingdom because the Kingdom family is a gift from God through Christ alone. We repent from our fleshly efforts that only get in the way, and we receive the gift. We repent from selfishness and isolation from others and from God. We turn our backs on the pursuit of riches and gain in this world in view of the riches that are in the heart of the Father for us. If leaving selfishness behind us proves to be hard then it is just a reflection of how far away we were from understanding how much Daddy God loves us and how much we truly need him! Father, we are pleased to be your kids!

BIBLICAL INSIGHT: Jesus teaches the disciples that the Kingdom will come down on them. They are to pray the Kingdom to come on earth as it is in Heaven. The Kingdom must be sought after now, and it must be realized in this world. When Jesus drove out the demons from someone who was terrorized by these evil forces then the Kingdom was said to have come on them in that moment. Jesus said that he conferred the Kingdom on his disciples just as his Father had conferred the Kingdom on him. The Kingdom is very, very near whenever the sons of God arrive. (Matthew 12:28; Luke 11:2; Luke 22:29-30)

OUR RESPONSE: The atmosphere in which the sons of God thrive is the Kingdom of God. The power of the Kingdom is all around and so we choose to live in it. We realize that we, too, are his disciples and that the Kingdom has been conferred on us as well. Because our relationship and favor with God can never be removed no matter where we go, we are now confident that wherever we step the authority of the Kingdom is present to drive out the work of demonic forces and bring deliverance and restoration to all that we touch. We agree with the Kingdom and expect it to affect our world.

BIBLICAL INSIGHT: As a place the Kingdom also exists in the future. As a place it is also right here and now. It is both here and it is to come. Only the Kingdom of God is eternal and without end. Looking forward to the outpouring of the Holy Spirit Jesus promises, "some who are standing here will not taste death before they see the Kingdom of God come with power."

Looking forward to the end of the age Jesus promises to celebrate with us at the beginning of the New Era Wedding Party. He says, "many will come from the east and the west, and will take their places at the feast with Abraham, Isaac and Jacob in the Kingdom of Heaven" (Matthew 8). It is during this future era—after the great separation of the sons from the impostors—that Jesus promises something amazing: "Then the righteous will shine like the sun in the Kingdom of their Father" (Matthew 13; Mark 14:25; Luke 19:11).

OUR RESPONSE: Jesus, we receive your promise of the future Kingdom. Jesus, we receive your promise of the present Kingdom. We proclaim your family invitation. We proclaim that in you, and you alone, there is eternal life. We have been restored to the Father forever, and now our hearts harmonize with yours—that no man should die but that everyone should have everlasting life. We are in the Kingdom now, and we will enjoy it with him forever. Father, make your children to shine now so that all may see us *shine like the sun in the Kingdom of our Father!*

ACT THREE:
40 Days More

After the Resurrection

Act Three opens and we are surrounded by the beauty and the power of the death and resurrection of Christ.

We can hear in the background John 12, in which Jesus says, "I tell you the truth, unless a kernel of wheat falls to the ground and dies, it remains only a single seed. But if it dies, it produces many seeds."

It is not a threat.

It is a promise.

Something huge is preparing to emerge.

The earth shakes and the temple curtain is torn.

The cross is pulled down, and Jesus is put in a stone tomb.

Wait.

Wait.

Wait.

The stone is rolled away and Jesus is alive!

The resurrection of Jesus is an overwhelming miracle, but Jesus didn't come out of the tomb and ascend straight into Heaven. The Scripture explains that over the next 40 days the disciples meet together and the resurrected Christ appears to them and teaches them in person! And what does he focus on? The Scripture says in the first chapter of Acts that for 40 days Jesus "showed himself to these [disciples] and gave many convincing proofs that he was alive. He appeared to them over a period of forty days and spoke about the Kingdom of God" (Acts 1).

If any of us could return from the dead and speak to those we love the most we would certainly focus on that which was most important. For Jesus what was most important was the message of the Kingdom of God.

After he had clarified the message of the Kingdom, Jesus tells them to go to Jerusalem and wait. He promises that the true power of the Kingdom would soon be unleashed. Something—or someone—would be announced.

The prophet Joel echoes in the walls of that room in Jerusalem where the disciples wait: "Then you will know that I am in Israel, that I am the LORD your God, and that there is no other; never again will my people be shamed. And afterward, I will pour out my Spirit on all people. Your sons and daughters will prophesy, your old men will dream dreams, your young men will see visions. Even on my servants, both men and women, I will pour out my Spirit in those days" (Joel 2).

ACT FOUR:
The Age of the Holy Spirit

The Arrival of the Holy Spirit

It is in the second chapter of Acts that we begin the final Act in our Kingdom theater. We see the disciples in a large room worshiping, praying for one another and waiting together for the promise: "When the day of Pentecost came, they were all together in one place. Suddenly a sound like the blowing of a violent wind came from Heaven and filled the whole house where they were sitting. They saw what seemed to be tongues of fire that separated and came to rest on each of them. All of them were filled with the Holy Spirit and began to speak in other tongues as the Spirit enabled them" (Acts 2).

As the Holy Spirit descends on each one like fire, we immediately realize how powerfully connected the Holy Spirit is to the message of the Kingdom of God. We remember Jesus, in John 14, speaking intimately with his disciples saying, "And I will ask the Father, and he will give you another Counselor to be with you forever—the Spirit of truth [...] I will not leave you as orphans."

He has not left us as orphans! He has not left us like children without parents! The Holy Spirit has come ... and now we can know God as our Father!

This outpouring on Pentecost was the end of life as orphans raised by the rules and management of an orphanage and the beginning of life as *empowered sons.*

It is no mistake that when the Spirit came he descended on the disciples in much the same way that the Spirit descended on Jesus when Jesus came up out of the waters of baptism. The drama and power of this moment spoke to the disciples clearly of the Father's love for them and his full acceptance of them into his heart. We can feel the power of the worship in that place. The whole room is filled with the sense of God's voice from Heaven saying, *You are my sons, and with you I am very well pleased!*

We can see now that if speaking in tongues is a sign of anything, it is certainly a sign that the Kingdom of God is not of this earth. Those who are filled with the power of God will do things and operate in things that do not seem normal in this world, and they will be never be fully understood by men.

Our minds are alive with the teaching from Romans 8:15 and following in which Paul explains, "for you did not receive a spirit that makes you a slave again to fear, but you received the Spirit of sonship. And by him we cry, 'Abba, Father.' The Spirit himself testifies with our spirit that we are God's children. Now if we are children, then we are heirs—heirs of God and co-heirs with Christ, if indeed we share in his sufferings in order that we may also share in his glory."

The Holy Spirit is the Spirit of adoption. He may empower us in many, many ways and reveal many things to us in our journey, but we can be absolutely sure of this:

- The Holy Spirit will reveal to us the Father's love!

- The Holy Spirit will convince us of our sonship!

- The Holy Spirit will make powerfully real our inheritance in Christ and empower us to live inside of him!

Now the scene changes and we see the disciples surrounded by onlookers. The atmosphere around the disciples and the people of God has suddenly changed. It has changed from powerful hope to powerful confidence—from patient waiting to powerful action. The Holy Spirit has changed the atmosphere in their lives to the atmosphere of the Kingdom of God. They stand up in a confidence they had never known before as the story in Acts 2 continues: "Then Peter stood up with the Eleven, raised his voice and addressed the crowd: 'Fellow Jews and all of you who live in Jerusalem, let me explain this to you; listen carefully to what I say...'" and he proclaims the salvation that was offered through Jesus Christ alone. Peter continues to preach confidently:

> God has raised this Jesus to life, and we are all witnesses of the fact. Exalted to the right hand of God, he has received from the Father the promised Holy Spirit and has poured out what you now see and hear [...] Therefore let all Israel be assured of this: God has made this Jesus, whom you crucified, both Lord and Christ.
>
> When the people heard this, they were cut to the heart and said to Peter and the other apostles, "Brothers, what shall we do?"
>
> Peter replied, "Repent and be baptized, every one of you, in the name of Jesus Christ for the forgiveness of your sins. And you will receive the gift of the Holy

Spirit. The promise is for you and your children and for all who are far off—for all whom the Lord our God will call."

Absolutely amazing.

Absolutely Kingdom.

This is how we know we are to be baptized in water in his name. We repent from our old life of working for righteousness, just as John the Baptist preached, and we join into Jesus' own family. We take on his name and we join with his message. It is the promise and arrival of the Holy Spirit that marks us as sons with absolute certainty.

The Kingdom of God Advances

The disciples continue in this simple, powerful message throughout the rest of the book of Acts, here are some excerpts.

• "But when they believed Philip as he preached the good news of the Kingdom of God and the name of Jesus Christ, they were baptized, both men and women."

• "Paul entered the synagogue and spoke boldly there for three months, arguing persuasively about the Kingdom of God."

• "From morning till evening he [Paul] explained and declared to them the Kingdom of God and tried to convince them about Jesus from the Law of Moses and from the Prophets."

• "Boldly and without hindrance he preached the Kingdom of God and taught about the Lord Jesus Christ."

Later, the words of Paul, in the first chapter of his letter to the Ephesians, come alive in light of the good news of the family kingdom:

Praise be to the God and Father of our Lord Jesus Christ, who has blessed us in the heavenly realms with every spiritual blessing in Christ. For he chose us in him before the creation of the world to be holy and blameless in his sight. In love he predestined us to be adopted as his sons through Jesus Christ, in accordance with his pleasure and will—to the praise of his glorious grace, which he has freely given us in the One he loves. In him we have redemption through his blood, the forgiveness of sins, in accordance with the riches of God's grace that he lavished on us with all wisdom and understanding. And he made known to us the mystery of his will according to his good pleasure, which he purposed in Christ [...] And you also were included in Christ when you heard the word of truth, the gospel of your salvation. Having believed, you were marked in him with a seal, the promised Holy Spirit, who is a deposit guaranteeing our inheritance until the redemption of those who are God's possession—to the praise of his glory.

It is so easy to hear in this passage the words we have already identified as God's family language: *Father, chose, adopted as sons, mystery, Holy Spirit,* and *inheritance.*

Paul was adamant about the Kingdom of God being neither a mere concept nor a new rule book, but rather it being the expression of the Holy Spirit in us. In Romans 14:17 he says, "For the Kingdom of God is not a matter of eating and drinking, but of righteousness, peace and joy in the Holy Spirit." Paul attacks the idea that by obeying Jewish laws and customs the Corinthian believers would somehow become better Christians. He knows they were trying to create their own righteousness again, and he slaps it down hard. Righteousness, peace, and joy are not things that can be created by man for man. We cannot build a system that will provide these things for us. These are the outworking of the Holy Spirit, who is always proving the arrival of the Kingdom of God.

In 1 Corinthians 4:12-21 Paul scolds some of the Corinthian believers for building cliques and prejudices in the Church and for listening to self-serving teachers. He makes a threatening promise to visit personally and demonstrate the power of God as their fathering apostle: "But I will come to you very soon, if the Lord is willing, and then I will find out not only how these arrogant people are talking, but what power they have. For the Kingdom of God is not a matter of talk but of power. What do you prefer? Shall I come to you with a whip, or in love and with a gentle spirit?" Again, this power is not something set in place by the traditions of men. The Spirit of God on his people is a supernatural demonstration of the arrival of the Kingdom of God. Paul expected to see that power wherever he worked.

Paul also speaks very clearly about the inheritance we have in the Kingdom of God as a spiritual inheritance for God's new family. In 1 Corinthians 15:15 he says, "I declare to you, brothers, that flesh and blood cannot inherit the Kingdom of God, nor does the perishable inherit the imperishable," and in Colossians 1:12-13, "giving thanks to the Father, who has qualified you to share in the inheritance of the saints in the Kingdom of light. For he has rescued us from the dominion of darkness and brought us into the Kingdom of the Son he loves [!]" Paul wanted to make sure that no one made the mistake of thinking the Kingdom of God was a kingdom of this world—it was one born of the Spirit and belonging to the spiritual realm.

The Kingdom in the Coming Age

At the end of this act we enter the prophetic drama of the Book of Revelation. In the first few chapters we are transported into the vision of John and we see a huge golden throne rising above everything else in Heaven. Creatures and beings of all shapes and sizes fill in around the throne and the front of the stage and look inward at a lamb that has just appeared and is standing on the throne. Revelation 5:6 begins:

> Then I saw a Lamb, looking as if it had been slain, standing in the center of the throne, encircled by the four living creatures and the elders. He had seven horns and seven eyes, which are the seven spirits of God sent out into all the earth. He came and took the scroll from the right hand of him who sat on the throne.
>
> And when he had taken it, the four living creatures and the twenty-four elders fell down before the Lamb. Each one had a harp and they were holding golden bowls full of incense, which are the prayers of the saints.

The textured voices of the elders fills the heavens as they sing to the Lamb on the throne:

> You are worthy to take the scroll and to open its seals, because you were slain, and with your blood you purchased men for God from every tribe and language and people and nation. You have made them to be a Kingdom and priests to serve our God, and they will reign on the earth.

Now we realize that we have been thoroughly included in the promises of the Kingdom of God. We are now living in the age of the Holy Spirit.

THE BIG THREE: The Simplicity of the Kingdom

The Kingdom is only complicated for those who haven't yet believed and been born again into the family of God. Many scholars fail to understand the Kingdom because they trust in the power of their own minds. They haven't seen the *family* or it would be simple for them. However, they have, unfortunately, produced incredibly complicated books on the Kingdom for hundreds of years. Some of the most confusing and difficult scholarly works on any shelf are the works of people trying to define and categorize and teacherize the message of the Kingdom of God. I do not recommend you read them. There is a beautiful simplicity in seeing the Kingdom for what it really is.

BIG FAT OBVIOUS KINGDOM TRUTH #1:

The Kingdom is family.

If children can receive it easily, then why would we ever believe that it belonged only to those with complex minds and great mental aptitude? Family is imparted by birth to everyone in the natural world and so it is in the spiritual world as well. It is only in family that every person from the oldest to the youngest, the weakest to the strongest, the most useful to the most broken, all find equal place and security. It is imparted directly through the miracle of birth or by the grace of adoption, and it can't be purchased by intellect or will; therefore...

BIG FAT OBVIOUS KINGDOM TRUTH #2:

The Kingdom is for sons.

Why do you think Jesus leans into his disciples after some of these Kingdom parable sessions and says with a smile, "Hey, fellas, you know that the Kingdom is already yours ... hint, hint."

Well, that was my paraphrase, but Mark 4:10 says, "When he was alone, the Twelve and the others around him asked him about the parables. He told them, 'The secret of the Kingdom of God has been given to you. But to those on the outside everything is said in parables.'" Can't you see him winking just a bit and leaning in with one elbow on his knee? He leans in again to his dear friends and disciples and says in Luke 12:32, "Do not be afraid, little flock, for your Father has been pleased to give you the kingdom."

No kidding.

It's absolutely wonderful to my ears! This is our perfect pastor, Jesus, taking care of us and watching over our souls. He looks into our eyes, he touches us on the shoulder, and he says in effect: Don't worry about discerning the weight of all these sayings. The Kingdom is already yours and that is what is important.

Jesus affirms that the Kingdom is for sons, and that sons are adopted by love. If the Kingdom could be imparted by knowledge or works, then he would have established a different kind of system altogether. He assures us that, like a good family in this world, the Kingdom is a safe and sure place for us. For slaves and orphans this message of the Kingdom is confusing, but even they can be transformed at any moment by receiving the Father's love. Whereas some only hear the parables about the Kingdom, we, the sons, actually live in it!

BIG FAT OBVIOUS KINGDOM TRUTH #3:

We enter the Kingdom by faith in Christ.

Jesus says, "Trust me."

When we do ... here comes the Kingdom.

Even after the disciples had devolved once again into asking about rank in the new Kingdom, Jesus still answers with astounding grace: "You are those who have stood by me in my trials. And I confer on you a kingdom, just as my Father conferred one on me, so that you may eat and drink at my table in my Kingdom and sit on thrones, judging the twelve tribes of Israel" (Luke 22:28-30).

In this passage, he addresses their question about internal rank by giving them an answer of extreme proportions; that is, as Kingdom sons they would rule and reign with him over everything, so they shouldn't worry about where they are on the totem pole! Some worry about where they are in rank, but sons learn to laugh at the idea.

Aaaak838f-akivd;alkdfjH! Yes! (That was me banging on the keyboard. I also pounded my fists on the table and yelled and laughed and yelled.)

The Kingdom *naturally belongs to the sons and we become sons by trusting in Christ.*

It is a miracle.

We call it salvation.

The Kingdom is not just a point in time. It goes on forever and ever.

We have received the Spirit of adoption as a gift, and we have been miraculously transfused with the blood of Christ. We share Kingdom DNA. We complete the requirement given to Nicodemus for entering the Kingdom because we really have been born again.

As for the entrance requirement in Matthew 7:21, "Not everyone who says to me, 'Lord, Lord,' will enter the Kingdom of Heaven, but only he who does the will of my Father who is in Heaven,"—sons are not intimidated. Before Christ changed us by the miracle of re-creation and filled us with the Holy Spirit, we could no more have accomplished the will of the Father than we could have jumped to the moon. But, now ... well, now it's a whole different story. God's will is already complete in us, and we are perfectly pleasing to him because we can say, *We are clothed with Christ.* Of course our righteousness exceeds that of the Pharisees because our rightness is not from our efforts, but from Christ, who wraps us up in his perfection.

When Dad looks at us he sees Jesus, so of course he is pleased with us. We walk inside his will and the same words with which he voiced his pleasure over Jesus when Jesus came up from the waters of the Jordan, and now these are the words he speaks over us: *These are my beloved sons, in whom I am very well pleased.*

Welcome into the Kingdom of God.

THE CHURCH

The Wife that Jesus Loves

I sat beside Bob Terrell years ago on the front row of a little fellowship in west Texas. I had just played a song for the gathering, and he was getting ready to take the stage and teach, probably on 1 John. I had just "retired" from a staff position at a local fellowship and had begun my experimental career as an musician and minister—sort of an arts missionary. He turned to me and said, "Ben, do you worry sometimes about where your provision [money] is going to come from?"

"Yes."

He said, "Well, you take care of the Bride and the Bridegroom will take care of you." The fellowship leaders introduced him and he moved up to the podium and began to teach. I just sat there thinking.

Now it is my turn, fifteen years later, to encourage you with the same question: Do you sometimes worry about your provision?

Well, remember this: Jesus loves his wife. If you love her and take care of her, you will certainly win his heart. This applies to everyone—not just experimental missionary types. Love the wife of Jesus, and you will win his heart.

I do not want the Bridegroom to ever overhear me slandering her. I also do not want to become complacent in my work to promote her health. I want to be known as a lover of the Bride in public and in private. As she matures I will compliment her on her beauty. When I read these words in Ephesians 4:29—"Do not let any unwholesome talk come out of your mouths, but only what is helpful for building others up according to their needs, that it may benefit those who listen"—I think of how my words affect her.

I want to be a graceful gift to the Bride that Jesus loves.

Let's think of it this way: If you come to my home and want to find favor with me, what might you do that will just about guarantee it?

Yes, that's it.

If you honor my wife and children, compliment them, encourage them, and help them in any way, I will notice. I will be compelled to give favor to you. I will provide for you in some way. Jesus will do the same, but his ability to provide knows no bounds.

The only people who will have trouble with this challenge to love are those who can't separate their ideas of the Church as a building where all the people meet and the Church as the people of God.

The Church is the people of God. She belongs to God. I am not a Church cynic because I believe that my complaints and disappointments with her are like my disappointments with my own family. My role is not to criticize or diminish but always to build up. I may criticize malfunctioning institutions because they don't let the Church be herself, but I don't waste too much time on it.

Bashing institutions has no great payoff.

Being a reformer of institutions is a very weak step towards helping the Church mature. If institutions could have perfected her, then they would have perfected her a long time ago. You see, many people have obsessed over and financed great and innovative organizations that were built for her service, but none of these efforts have done what we hoped for.

Want to know why?

Family only matures according to family rules. Family does not mature according to organizational rules. When the hearts of fathers and sons return to one another we mature, but we do not mature when the hearts of employees turn toward their managers. When sons commit to loving one another we mature, but we don't mature when organizational members commit to work together to complete a task. When we receive the grace gifts of people more than we strive for the grace gifts of ideas, then we mature. When we see the Holy Spirit as the great family builder and receive the baptism of the Holy Spirit as sons instead of seeing him as an optional power enhancer, then we mature.

Dear believers, we must put all our effort into being the family—the Kingdom people—God has created us to be. And the Church will then grow and mature as the natural byproduct.

Listen: A tree is to a forest as a son is to the Church. If we put several trees together in a field, we call it a forest. If we put several sons together in loving relationship, we call it the Church. This is why we don't have to try and build the Church, and it is why we were never called to try. We are called to receive the Spirit of adoption and to mature as his sons. When we love one another according to our new nature and we grow together, then we are the Church.

Easy.

The Church is nothing more than the identifiable people of God connecting together in love as one family on this earth.

Jesus loves the Church.

Seeing the Church

I'll say it again: The Church is the people of God—*not anything else.*

The Church is not the meetings. The Church is not the buildings. To think so is craziness. Unfortunately, however, we have shifted from a people-only understanding of the Church to system-and-building understanding.

Our fixation on promoting Church meetings is connected to the way we have defined the Church. In short, we adopted the idea of Church as a structure—a form—and so now we obsess over getting people into it. It has depreciated our heart for evangelism and has made many of us very, very tired.

Sure, it is a basic human instinct to build homes, towns, and fortresses. That is not a problem. It is a problem when we confuse our home *with a house.* One is real and relational, and one is temporary and impersonal. "Home," to quote the cliche, "is where the heart is," and it is found in the eyes of our family. A house is made of mere wood and stone.

When we shift away from understanding the Church as the people of God, then our focus shifts right along with it. It goes something like this:

- We must meet together! (Great!)

- We must build great meetings! (Really?)

- We must have buildings worthy of our meetings! (Oh, no!)

- The Church is a place where we go to have great meetings! (Craziness.)

Do you see how easy it is to slide into craziness? Though we had great intentions, the houses we have built have become prisons for the people of God. They have locked us in, and they have locked others out. Our only hope is to rediscover the Kingdom of God and redefine the Church as people.

Unfortunately, to really understand the depth of this pathology—this mental sickness—we can't confine our observations to the Christian obsession with physical buildings alone. That would be a gross reduction of the true width and breadth of modern Christian institutionalism. Institutionalism is when something meant to live free is confined within a static, non-living system. We have not only called a place—instead of a people—the Church, but we have also allowed our imagination of Church to settle inside of the good ideas and static structures of our traditions. We have now come to see "the way we do it" as Church.

We show this as our working definition for Church by marking our territories of doctrinal influence and staking our traditional claims. *This is my Church. This is our way. That is their way.* We prove it when we grow fond of words like attendance, growth, liberal, traditional, mine, yours, location, relevant, emergent, progressive, we, them ... and many more. We are all being reduced by this categorical, territorial language. It reduces us first in our imaginations, then as individuals and ultimately as a connected family.

As a matter of fact, since these words have been successfully killing the idea of family for quite some time we are now left searching for new words that we can understand ourselves with. Many of us have been opting for the word *community* as a working replacement. Community, in this new vocabulary, happens when people live close together or even in the same home. Community happens when people share meals and time and conversations. Community, in this modern usage, covers almost every healthy activity people can do with one another in close proximity, but we all know that community is no replacement for family. It is easy to see that community flows effortlessly from family, but family is not, in any way, the natural byproduct of community. Community is an inferior replacement for understanding the Church as a family, but it has been needed because we have lowered ourselves into much-less-than-family institutions both on the ground and in our minds.

When we divide the Church into pieces and parts based on doctrine, traditions, and buildings we reveal our inferior imaginations. We have often seen the Church as little more than an organization built to defend the greater Christian ideas from the lesser ideas, and so down we go into classes and divisions.

The Church is not a collection of great ideas. We must repent from reducing her to this!

The Church is the beautiful people of God.

God's people are not cattle. They are not to be divided and classed according to their assent to specific ideas or adherence to a system of traditions. However, we have become famous for marking lines on the ground and herding the believer-livestock into our stalls. This separation has brought so much prejudice that now we need schools to justify the spiritual meaning of all these divisions. This caste system will never be the glory of the beautiful people of God, yet author after author and speaker after speaker hit the sales-trail in hopes of selling their latest version of the new-and-improved Church. This is nothing but immature promotion of division in the family.

We are a family who are meant to be reconciled together, and we must pray for reconcilers to take courage and lead!

The Beautiful Church is One

When we hear the appeal to discover the beautiful Church we are not going to lower our minds and obsess over narrow ideas that only addresses her form. For instance, it would be misguided to promote the small Church as the best one. It would be misguided to believe the modern Church with new worship styles as the most effective one. And it would painfully prejudiced to cling to the notion that only the ancient Church with liturgy and tradition contain the best things about her.

Foolishness.

Remember, Jesus only used the word *Church* twice in all of the Gospels: once when he claims it as his own to build in Matthew 16, and once when he requires reconciliation among its members in Matthew 18. Jesus spoke of the Church like a man standing near a huge grouping of trees can point to the forest. It is obvious. It is clear to see. It takes no striving for him to identify her as the people of God. Her beauty is intrinsic just as each person is intrinsically beautiful. God sees the beauty of his people individually, and then together as his family. This should be our vision as well.

My wife is not beautiful because of what she does or what she wears or where she sits. Her very essence is beautiful, and she is most beautiful to me when she is at perfect rest in who she is. Jesus feels the same way about his Church, and his love for her does not change based on whether she is working hard, or lying perfectly at rest in his love. His love does not change if she is meeting in a stadium or in a home, whether she plays electric guitars or pipe organs, or whether she wears an old dress or enjoys a brand new one. He simply loves her.

In modern Christian life it is talk about the form, the style, and the function of the Church that dominates our books and our conversations. Let's stop obsessing over the very things that Christ made absolutely no effort to entertain and start obsessing over reconciling with the people in our view. Reconciliation and forgiveness are the only directive words Jesus ever spoke regarding the dynamics of our life together as the Church. This says something important and we should take note. Matthew 18 is not first a guide on how to be reconciled, it is first and foremost a directive *to be reconciled together as one family.*

Seeing the Church

Let's take a few moments to lift our imagination of the Church so that we can be clear and encouraging to one another and so that we can learn to see her as Christ sees her. This will help us avoid any accidental diminishment of the Bride or any unwholesome talk that might come out of our mouths and harm her. Here we will choose to be brief and scripturally to the point as we establish our new vision for the Church:

The Church belongs to Jesus.

He claims her in Matthew 16 when He says to Peter, "on this rock I will build my Church, and the gates of Hades will not prevail against it." The Church is not ours and does not belong to men in any century. We should repent for ever using the words "my" or "your" when trying to identify the Church or any individual fellowships that we have learned to call Church. These words make us seem petty to the world, and they breed division between us.

The Church is the people of God.

She has never been a building or an organization, and we should repent for *stupidifying* the word by using it in this way almost constantly. There is no reference in all of Scripture to prove otherwise, and we must stop worshipping idols by constantly referring to these man-made things as the Church that Jesus died to build. He did not die for wood and mortar; he died for his people. His wife is not a stone edifice but a collection of living stones. For this reason we never "go to Church."

There is only one Church.

She may be identified as the people of God in a city or region that meet together like *the Church at Antioch* or *the Church in their house* or *the Church of God that is in Corinth*. These phrases are clear; however, they identify only one Church who happens to be gathering in different places. It is the one Church who in part can be seen in Antioch, or who, in another part, can be seen in your home. There has never been more than one Church, and to even consider that there has been is just nuts. Jesus claims one Church, and she may be found in many, many places both big and small throughout the world. It is only with this understanding that we can use the plural word "Churches" like it is used in the Book of Revelation. We can recognize the Church that meets at First Baptist's building, but we will not continue to recognize the First Baptist Church as though it is a different Church than the forty-seven other gatherings in the same city. The difference is not subtle. Jesus is not a polygamist.

The one Church is a multi-faceted beauty.

As his people we understand our nature as the Church in different, beautiful analogies, each having a unique revelation for us. These include the *temple*, the *body*, the *bride*, and the *family*. Each of these word pictures speaks to our nature and our relationship to God. The *temple* speaks to our sacred purpose and the presence of the Holy Spirit. The *body* speaks to our work in this world, and our inseparable relationship with Christ, the head. The *bride* speaks of our value in the eyes of our Lord, and his great passion and pursuit of us. The *family* speaks of the very nature of God as the Trinity and the nature of our Kingdom DNA code. None of these give support for division in the Church based on style, race, doctrine, or history, and so now we are committed to ignoring the bigotries of men. We ignore all of them. There is no such thing as a black Church, or a house Church, or a liturgical Church. There are black people who are in the Church, there is Church that meets in homes, and there are some in the Church who enjoy liturgy, but this is a huge difference in language and belief.

We must be committed to building the multifaceted people of God without prejudice.

The Church has only one foundation.

The first foundation of the Church, the stuff that gives it stability, is Christ himself who is the Chief Cornerstone. Jesus is the unmoving, eternal anchor point from which the whole Church is fit to and built upon. He is the plumb-line and the structural basis. He is the beginning of the Church and he is the final word on its growth and fulfillment.

The second layer of foundation are the apostles and prophets. According to Ephesians 2:20 and 4:11, Jesus gives us the apostles and prophets as people that build stability into the Church. (He also gives us teachers, pastors, and evangelists to build us up, but these are not mentioned as foundational.) Apostles and prophets are expressions of his own foundational grace. These are real people, not just concepts. They are real people who serve underneath the family as load-bearing servants. They architect and they foresee. They plan and they promote. What do they plan and promote? *Always* the family of God and *never* the form or the organization. They proclaim what is coming, and they require everything to be properly related to Jesus the Chief Cornerstone. This was true of the prophets before Jesus, and the Twelve Apostles of the Lamb, and the prophets and apostles of the first century Church, and it is still true today. Any Church expression, local or translocal, that is not built on these foundations is destined to be structurally unsound, unstable, and will eventually come to ruin the more weight is placed upon it.

Jesus' gifts to the Church are people.

The ministry gifts—who are first the apostles, second the prophets, and third the teachers, pastors, and evangelists—are all given to build up the Church by building up every believer to do works of service and to mature in Christ. They are not called to build organizations or doctrinal fortresses, but rather they are called to give themselves away to serve the people of God. According to Ephesians 4 and 1 Corinthians 12, these leadership graces equip the saints; they do not strive to build a better organization. Furthermore, as directed in Titus 1:5, elders are to be appointed by the apostles to lead the local gatherings of the Church. The "order" of the Church is founded in actual people full of the grace who are connecting together, building one another, and submitting ultimately to Christ. It is not established on doctrines or traditions, and there is no other way to imagine the health and maturity of the Church that Jesus loves.

The Church is always the people.

Church uniquely identifies the people of God on the earth, not the structures of organization or the traditions of men. We are, according to the Greek translation of the word Church, the "called out ones" of God who love to gather together because we are family, not because we all agree with each other about everything. The word *Church* is always used in any New Testament teaching to identify us—the people of God—and our function in the earth. The word is not used to identify our eternal life to come because the Church is about the practical here-and-now understanding of who we are in Christ, set apart from others in this world who have not yet been adopted as sons. In the next life, I could suppose, we won't need to see ourselves as "set apart from others." *Church* identifies who we are for one another right now.

The Church is the people of God wherever they are.

I realize this may almost seem repetitious, even remedial, at this point, but it bears a moment of emphasis. If a family doesn't need a house to be a family, then the Church doesn't need a meeting to be the Church. The sons of God—wherever they are —are always the Church. They can be on a mission endeavor or resting on the porch. They can hold hands in person, or they can connect over the phone. They can be in a huge worship meeting or driving together in a car. They can be in an international relief hub or in a local prison. They are the Church everywhere.

Being the Church

Jesus has already claimed us as his Church, so let's receive it and be who we were reborn to be. Let's be God's beautiful family! Why should we worry about the future of the Church? If we pour the best of ourselves into our natural families, we have to let go and trust that they will grow and do well. We can do the same with the Church that God gives us to love. We don't need to control or design. We can just pour out our love on each other and trust that Jesus alone will build it.

Can you leave that job to him?

Remember Matthew 16:18 when Jesus says, "And I tell you that you are Peter, and on this rock I will build my Church, and the gates of Hades will not overcome it."

He has called us to build each other up, but he has not called us to build his own family. Building each other up is a radically different proposition than the work required to oversee and direct the growth of a family. Jesus will make all the plans necessary for his Church to grow. All we have to do is love the people he has given to us the best that we can.

Our small part in the life of the Church is to love those within our reach. He is always directing us to love, to pastor, to encourage, and to prophecy in order to build other people up, but he is not trying to turn over the architecture to us. We are called to cooperate with him and, like happy workers, to obey the constant and clear vision of our master builder.

Now, Paul does say in 1 Corinthians 3:10: "By the grace God has given me, I laid a foundation as an expert builder, and someone else is building on it. But each one should be careful how he builds." We might think this sounds contradictory. I don't think it is. Paul is speaking in a metaphor that always fills an apostle's heart. He is not assuming the authority that Christ has to build the Church, but he is aware of his own grace to be a foundation laying leader. Apostles are foundation layers and fathers. Apostles are always laying foundations and creating a space that is clear and level for the people of God to build on together, but they would never assume Christ's authority and try to direct the growth of the family on their own.

What is the foundation that they lay?

It is always Jesus.

Every leadership grace, including pastors, prophets, teachers, and evangelists, given to the Church expresses the heart and purposes of Christ in leadership, but we all have an expression of Christ to share! Every believer has a portion of grace, that is, an expression of Christ that they can share with those around them. The Church is where we enjoy being who we are in him as sons and sharing ourselves with one another. It is the living, breathing example of one another love. We don't have to proclaim the Church in order to see it come to life because when we come together around Jesus *we simply are the Church.* Oh, my friends, if we could only put down all the tools and monies and energies we put into trying to make the Church a certain way and just rest in being the Church, how full and wonderful our lives would be. This is a call to stop promoting mega-Church, or small Church, or relaxed Church, or formal Church, or traditional Church—et cetera ad infinitum ad nauseum. Promoting these things will not lead to anything other than divisions and prejudices and immaturity.

God has not called us to promote our best idea of the Church; he has called us to promote and proclaim the Kingdom of God.

We can simply *be the Church.*

Claiming the Church

Jesus proclaimed the Kingdom. Jesus claimed the Church.

He spoke of the Kingdom as a force, a way, a reality that we could release, enjoy, and find power for living in. He looked out over the future of his new people, saw our faces, and said, *This is my Church.* He claimed the Church like we might claim our own family.

We have permission, I believe, to look out over the fields of our lives and claim just what Christ claims. We can claim the people of God around us as our new family and then we can call ourselves the Church. By opening our eyes and listing the names of the believing people around us we are actually bringing the Church to life, and it will be the kind of Church that we can live with. Church, for us, may never have to be any larger than this list. We might imagine the Church in the whole world, but we are finite creatures so we can only take up our responsibility in the portion of the Church that we can see and call by name.

The reason I am making this point here is crucial. Many people passively move through life with no intent to claim anyone. They move from this place to that place, from this fellowship to that one, from this event to another and they never lay hold to any relationship and call it permanent. These same people don't have a clue how to enjoy the Church because they have fundamentally failed to see that the Church is only people and that the Church is theirs to claim. The most common complaints from Christians who slide though life without claiming others as family are: I don't have friends. I don't feel welcome in the Church. I feel alone.

Take out a pen. Write down the names of the believers around you with whom you have some kind of personal connection. Say aloud, "This is the Church for me."

THE TRADITIONS OF MEN

A Fight

Here is the section of our book where it is acceptable to use references like Catholic, Protestant, Baptist, House Church, Mega-Church, Armenian, Calvinist, The Celtic Way, Anglican, Independent Charismatic, Missional Community, Organic, Reformed, Orthodox, Progressive, Emergent, Traditional, Liturgical, Evangelical, just to name a few. These are all the creative ways we—with feet of clay and minds of dust—have chosen to identify ourselves and divide ourselves from others who are following Christ. We have given these classes formal names. These are the well-financed ways we have divided ourselves from one another.

Congratulations, Church, for creating and sustaining the multiple personality disorder that has plagued us for generations. So, how has it been working out for you?

That was rhetorical.

I know that proposing mental disease seems awkward. Did I go too far? I know it can make us all very uneasy. Most of us have rationalized these divisions and we don't dare question them anymore. When someone does question them and when someone might even propose that the system is sick, our instinct is to step back and say: Wait, aren't you touching something sacred that we shouldn't touch?

It is no wonder we get nervous. There are whole classes of book-writing, university-leading, and scholarly fraternities that have existed for centuries whose only purpose has been to prove the legitimacy of these divisions. This kind of human effort is designed only to make us feel justified in sustaining our disease.

It makes me sick.

It has been making us all sick.

Men who have been impressed with their own righteousness have been carrying out secret experiments in the petri dishes of doctrinal refinement, and they conduct the cloning of obedient leadership classes in the back rooms of seminaries and leadership summits. It doesn't seem right that in a small paperback featuring goldfish and aquariums this not-so-secret-society would be challenged to a fight ... but here we go.

Put Family First

First, let's take a moment together to hear Jesus' own words challenging the traditions of men, and then, later, we will broaden our perspective with two clear statements from the writings of Paul. I make this commitment to you now: I have no intent of bringing harm or harsh words to anyone who is struggling with the tradition that surrounds their own journey. I want to help you, and I do not want to burn anything down that would hurt you.

In Mark 7 and in Matthew 15, this story is told of Jesus confronting the traditions of men and the Pharisees:

> The Pharisees and some of the teachers of the law who had come from Jerusalem gathered around Jesus and saw some of his disciples eating food with hands that were "unclean," that is, unwashed. (The Pharisees and all the Jews do not eat unless they give their hands a ceremonial washing, holding to the tradition of the elders. When they come from the marketplace they do not eat unless they wash. And they observe many other traditions, such as the washing of cups, pitchers and kettles.) So the Pharisees and teachers of the law asked Jesus, "Why don't your disciples live according to the

tradition of the elders instead of eating their food with 'unclean' hands?"

At first reading of this passage, I am not sure why Jesus would take such a hard line with these leaders. The fact that the Jews observed certain rituals doesn't really seem like a real problem. My mom always told me to wash my hands before dinner. What's the big deal?

Well, the key is the foundational problem Jesus was pointing out. Jesus came to proclaim the Kingdom and the Kingdom as family. What these Pharisees were doing was harming the family and keeping people from receiving the Kingdom. Worse, they were teaching others to trust in things that were not Kingdom at all: their traditions. Jesus replies to the leaders and is painfully direct: "Isaiah was right when he prophesied about you hypocrites; as it is written: 'These people honor me with their lips, but their hearts are far from me. They worship me in vain; their teachings are but rules taught by men.' You have let go of the commands of God and are holding on to the traditions of men" (Mark 7:6-8).

Ouch.

Jesus took the correction beyond just an awkward moment and into the realm of serious rebuke. Jesus quotes Isaiah 29:13 word for word and sticks it right to these super-leaders. Remember, these guys may have already had Isaiah 29 strapped to their arms or foreheads as they were known to do to show their commitment to Scripture. They loved the Scripture. At least they loved what loving the Scripture gave them in terms of power and authority. It gave them a special place. But it was not a place in *family*. Jesus cut straight to the heart—their hearts—and accused them of double motives and of leaving God for the sake of tradition. He accused them of having a value system that was completely upside down.

Discerning their mistake was very simple. Jesus knew they didn't really love Dad, because if they did they would show love and concern for all of his people. Instead these guys brought division and prejudice everywhere they went. They made others look less righteous and made themselves out to be more righteous because of their teachings and adherence to what they claimed to be God's will. Their ultimate offense was not their pride but their work of dividing and confusing the people that God loves. We have learned that God's will is for us to come close to him as family. These men were not interested in coming close to anything but more self-promotion inside of their traditions, and Jesus knew it.

Jesus went on in Mark 7 to give a specific example of how their traditions had been used to dishonor—yes, you guessed it —the family:

> You have a fine way of setting aside the commands of God in order to observe your own traditions! For Moses said, "Honor your father and your mother," and, "Anyone who curses his father or mother must be put to death." But you say that if a man says to his father or mother: "Whatever help you might otherwise have received from me is Corban" (that is, a gift devoted to God), then you no longer let him do anything for his father or mother. Thus you nullify the word of God by your tradition that you have handed down. And you do many things like that.

It is not a coincidence that Jesus brings his correction right to the heart of how they disrespected the sacred beauty of the natural family to prove his point. He says in essence: if you can't love your natural family, then you can't be trusted with spiritual family.

He caught them on a technicality in their interpretation of the original command in order to arrest their attention, but he indicted them on a sweeping heart crime: they had twisted the very words of the Scripture to justify abusing their own families.

Listen: Any tradition that we practice that brings harm in any way to our natural families has no place in the heart of God. This includes obsessions over meetings that replace quality time with our children. It includes replacing the value of family rest with a constant need to be available to the needs of the institution. It includes ignoring certain age groups in an effort to be super hip and trendy. If we choose to preserve our tradition to the neglect of our natural family then we, too, are hypocrites.

Why? Because hypocrites are people that say one thing and do another. What really was the Pharisees' hypocrisy? Was it just a technical loophole they created in a single teaching? Was it their inability to understand Scripture?

No.

The Pharisees said they knew the heart of God, but they taught things that did not build the family of God. We have clearly seen the heart of God *is* family, but they did not. This was their crime, and this was their most offensive spiritual hypocrisy to Jesus.

We need to stop and take account of our own traditions in this light. The Pharisees had bought into some mental and doctrinal real estate that had become so important to them that they could no longer see beyond their own fences and hear the words of the Father. They could no longer see his family. They could not, therefore, receive the Kingdom.

Nothing is more dangerous to the Kingdom than men who must hold to, promote, and defend their traditions above all else.

Jesus continues in Mark 7 to explain to the disciples and everyone standing around how these traditions had turned the will of God upside down, or, more literally, inside out:

> Again Jesus called the crowd to him and said, "Listen to me, everyone, and understand this. Nothing outside a man can make him 'unclean' by going into him. Rather, it is what comes out of a man that makes him 'unclean.'"
>
> After he had left the crowd and entered the house, his disciples asked him about this parable. "Are you so dull?" he asked. "Don't you see that nothing that enters a man from the outside can make him 'unclean'? For it doesn't go into his heart but into his stomach, and then out of his body." (In saying this, Jesus declared all foods "clean.") He went on: "What comes out of a man is what makes him 'unclean.' For from within, out of men's hearts, come evil thoughts, sexual immorality, theft, murder, adultery, greed, malice, deceit, lewdness, envy, slander, arrogance and folly. All these evils come from inside and make a man 'unclean.'"

The Pharisees and even the disciples struggled to understand, and Jesus was frustrated at this point that his own men were still not getting it. Here it is in two points:

First, all righteousness comes down from God alone and never from our actions. It is a gift. Period.

Second, righteousness is evidenced in the lives of people when they *love one another!!*

Do you see, dear reader, that putting bacon in your body does nothing to harm the family of God? Do you also see that all these things that Jesus listed: evil thoughts, sexual immorality, theft, murder, adultery, greed, malice, deceit, lewdness, envy, slander, arrogance and folly, are all direct attacks on the sacredness of relationship? Can you see that these sins are are a direct attack on family health? They are the opposite of Kingdom life.

If we camp out in a tradition and build fences around it in order to find our safety there, it will soon limit our ability to see the heart of God. We should not look for righteousness—the feeling of being okay—in traditions. God's heart is to give us our righteousness as a gift and to help us love him and love one another. These simple requirements are boiled down to the heart of love: "Love the Lord your God with all your heart and with all your soul and with all your strength," and "Love your neighbor as yourself" (Deuteronomy 6:5; Leviticus 19:18). Somehow the heart that does not rest in the love of God will always turn to the creation of traditions and begin to trust them, love them, and live completely inside of them. It is sad and destructive, and it is still the rule today.

In the very next passage in Mark 7 Jesus heals a woman's demon-possessed daughter, a foreigner not in line to receive any blessing from God according to Jewish tradition. He says again to those who cling to tradition and do not have a heart for the family of God: Your priorities are not the same as mine. Jesus was about every sacred person, but they were about preserving divisions and promoting their superiority. Jesus was about his family, but they were about forms and ideas.

We are called to make a choice.

Worship What is Worthy

In Matthew 12 another story is told of how Jesus took on the traditions of men as they relate to observing the Sabbath:

> At that time Jesus went through the grainfields on the Sabbath. His disciples were hungry and began to pick some heads of grain and eat them. When the Pharisees saw this, they said to him, "Look! Your disciples are doing what is unlawful on the Sabbath."
>
> He answered, "Haven't you read what David did when he and his companions were hungry? He entered the house of God, and he and his companions ate the consecrated bread—which was not lawful for them to do, but only for the priests. Or haven't you read in the Law that on the Sabbath the priests in the temple desecrate the day and yet are innocent? I tell you that one greater than the temple is here. If you had known what these words mean, 'I desire mercy, not sacrifice,' you would not have condemned the innocent. For the Son of Man is Lord of the Sabbath."

Remember, Jesus is well aware that he is proclaiming the Kingdom and that he is the King. When he reveals the Kingdom it always creates an opportunity to show that he rules everything, and that ultimate reality is in his wake. Many who trust in tradition continue to find this hard to swallow because for them, ultimate reality is found in conforming to a system created by men. Many actually worship their traditions before they worship God.

Jesus commands us to get our worship pointed in the right direction.

When the King is in our midst we don't bow down to his photograph—we bow down directly to the King. When the

Lord of the Sabbath is in your presence you don't try to prove to him that you rest in a more righteous way than others—you lay down and rest directly toward him. You rest in his presence and worship him.

The Pharisees' tradition had blinded them from seeing Jesus, just as ours can blind us today. Even if a tradition was created with benevolent hearts and helpful aspirations, we can't lean on it and expect it to provide for us. We can only lean on God. To lean on tradition is to lean on a pseudo-reality, and when Jesus shows up he will tear it down every time. He does this not to prove an intellectual point. He does this because he desires us to lean on him. He wants to be near to us.

This is why Jesus so emphatically tells the best and the brightest in Jerusalem who had learned to lean on the greatness and sacredness of Herod's temple, "Destroy this temple, and I will raise it again in three days" (John 2:19). Can't you hear him saying, "You can lean on this nice building if you want to, but I want you to lean on me. When I am resurrected you will see how foolishly temporary earthly temples really are." Jesus just had no sense of humor when it came to men turning their backs on the God who created them in order to worship and trust in things they built with their own hands.

It was because he could see the way it hurt them: It kept them from receiving the Kingdom of God.

You see, we destroy sacredness when we assign it to earthly things. Jesus was the most sacred element in all of the world, but these professional religious folks could not see him. They had assigned sacredness to things. They could only see what they had learned to trust in— namely, their own tradition.

Why do you think that the arrival of Jesus in any supernatural manifestation like healing, tongues, and prophecy is so threatening to staunch tradition-worshipers today?

It is because these and other spiritual manifestations are a direct threat to their positions of safety inside of their non-spiritual traditions. Every vibration of the Holy Spirit's power is a promise to tear down man-made sacred things—the sacredness of "this is how we do it."

Lord, please shake it.

Make People the Priority

Matthew 12 continues and we see just how twisted the minds of the religious can become. When you read this passage, think on how little value they gave the crippled man as they put Jesus to this foolish test:

> Going on from that place, he went into their synagogue, and a man with a shriveled hand was there. Looking for a reason to accuse Jesus, they asked him, "Is it lawful to heal on the Sabbath?" He said to them, "If any of you has a sheep and it falls into a pit on the Sabbath, will you not take hold of it and lift it out? How much more valuable is a man than a sheep! Therefore it is lawful to do good on the Sabbath." Then he said to the man, "Stretch out your hand." So he stretched it out and it was completely restored, just as sound as the other. But the Pharisees went out and plotted how they might kill Jesus.

The priority of the Kingdom is the beauty of people—the people of God's heart. Those who trust in the traditions of men are those whose priorities are on something—anything—other than caring for people. Isn't it is just ludicrous that Jesus would even have to say something as obvious as *men are more important than animals?* Fair warning: People that have conflicted feelings about a cripple man being healed are not safe people to be around.

The mind that turns away from God and begins to trust in its own creation is a sick mind that believes in an upside down world. Its sickness becomes a mental disease which destroys. It first destroys the eyes so that we cannot see the truth of family, and then it destroys our hearts and takes our very life. The blackness that follows sounds like this: "But the Pharisees went out and plotted how they might kill Jesus." This kind of disease was deadly for Jesus, and it will certainly be dangerous for us.

This upside down mindset is still working in our world today. We still lean on and trust traditions to make us feel okay about ourselves instead of leaning on Christ alone. We even prioritize things like style, human governments, and the environment as more important than people. Our traditions have brought division, judgement, and prejudices that divide the family of God.

It is time to repent.

We must put an end to it. We must at least put an end to it in our own spheres of influence. We must make people the priority.

Avoid Radicalism

At this point, I would like to treat some of the thoughts I suspect are already surfacing in your mind about burning down buildings or raging against denominations. I want to pause and make sure we understand what kind of revolutionary Jesus was before we decide on a hot course of action.

It is true that in Mark 2 Jesus seems to be doing everything in opposition to the traditions and expectations of men. For example, he sees the faith of a man who was lowered through the roof and he pronounces his sins forgiven and heals him. The traditionalists were appalled at the very idea that he would forgive a man's sins. Also, he goes down to a lake and calls Levi, a tax collector and the last person on anyone's list to become a disciple of a Rabbi, to follow him. Furthermore, he has dinner with Levi and his friends who were all, according to traditionalists, unworthy types and "sinners." Yet he gives these men honor and says, "It is not the healthy who need a doctor, but the sick. I have not come to call the righteous, but sinners" (Mark 2:17).

On yet another occasion, he turns to the Pharisees and tells them that the tradition of fasting does not apply to him or his disciples because fasting literally belongs to him: "'Look, why are they doing what is unlawful on the Sabbath?' he answered, 'Have you never read what David did when he and his companions were hungry and in need? In the days of Abiathar the high priest, he entered the house of God and ate the consecrated bread, which is lawful only for priests to eat. And he also gave some to his companions.' Then he said to them, 'The Sabbath was made for man, not man for the Sabbath. So the Son of Man is Lord even of the Sabbath'" (Mark 2:24-28).

Again, the Sabbath belonged to Jesus, but the Pharisees wanted to belong to the Sabbath.

So we know that Jesus was definitely radical. Jesus did not go with the popular flow. But let's make sure we understand why:

Jesus was reordering the nature of things. And this new order was the Kingdom of God. He was taking the time to redefine for these religious men what was really true—what was truly real. He was making clear the Kingdom reality.

Please take this to heart. Jesus did not rock the boat just to watch people scramble for lifejackets. He did not act like an non-comformist just to prove he was a revolutionary. His goal was not to create shock in the minds of traditionalists. Nor was he just trying to wake people up with radical words and actions. This is very important to understand or you, dear reader, might take flight on a journey that was never intended for you. His interest was not in offending anyone. He loved even the Pharisees without prejudice.

Jesus may have been a radical, but he did not suffer from radicalism. Radicalism is the commitment always to be radical. This commitment is weak, and it is not in the heart of Christ. It is not to be our hearts, either.

Again, Jesus' actions were simply to bring Kingdom order wherever he went. The reality of the Kingdom of God he proclaimed was so opposite from the reality of the religious that it stung them. For these leaders the rebuke had to be a hard correction because they were 180 degrees off course.

When he taught he simply re-organized the world around him according to the rule of the Kingdom of God. If that seemed upside down and revolutionary to traditionalists, then that was just the result of their backwards minds. Jesus proclaimed the ultimate authority of the Kingdom of God as the eternal reality and the temporal nature of everything else, exposing that men had developed ideas that were contrary to the Kingdom. He flowed gracefully on the power and truth of the Kingdom when he worked miracles, and it shook the world because the world was off balance, not him. So let's be clear: We are not called to shake up or destroy traditions in any way. We are called to proclaim the Kingdom of God. In *this way* we follow Jesus.

Some people we meet will be very close to the Kingdom, and some will be living in opposition to it. Whether or not they practice a particular tradition may have no bearing on their agreement with the Kingdom. We can't generalize our discernment for each person on whether they go to a certain fellowship or whether they were raised in a certain tradition. That kind of spiritual profiling doesn't work.

Everywhere we go as sons of the Kingdom we will, like Jesus, re-order the values, the priorities, and the very tone of the spiritual atmosphere by proclaiming the Kingdom of God. It is our nature as sons to do so.

Under a Spell

Our call in God has never been to protect and promote the traditions of men. The apostle Paul identifies this fork in our collective road when he says in Galatians 1:14, "I was advancing in Judaism beyond many Jews of my own age and was extremely zealous for the traditions of my fathers, but when God, who set me apart from birth and called me by his grace, was pleased to reveal his Son in me so that I might preach him among the Gentiles, I did not consult any man." Paul is saying that our future in God is not handed to us from history or tradition, but that it comes when we encounter him personally. The fork in our road is the decision to cling to tradition or to cling to God.

I think we can say, then, that any tradition or teaching that says to us "trust me for your future" instead of "trust God" is going to be rebuked by the Kingdom instincts that are alive in us. In Colossians 2:8 Paul writes with some force, "See to it that no one takes you captive through hollow and deceptive philosophy, which depends on human tradition and the basic principles of this world rather than on Christ."

This deceptive human tradition is one that leads us away from his admonition in the verses preceding: "just as you received Christ Jesus as Lord, continue to live in him, rooted and built up in him, strengthened in the faith as you were taught, and overflowing with thankfulness" (Colossians 2:6-7). We know that we can add nothing to our present walk with him that does not reflect how we began in him, and we began with a childlike faith! We received him by faith. Now we walk in him by faith. We are to continue on in him alone, trusting that he began our transformation and he will complete it. We do not need anything else added to this simple truth. The things we try to add to our faith are called "the traditions of men."

Paul goes on to make this rejection of the principles of this world very specific when he adds,

> Therefore do not let anyone judge you by what you eat or drink, or with regard to a religious festival, a New Moon celebration or a Sabbath day. These are a shadow of the things that were to come; the reality, however, is found in Christ. Do not let anyone who delights in false humility and the worship of angels disqualify you for the prize. Such a person goes into great detail about what he has seen, and his unspiritual mind puffs him up with idle notions. He has lost connection with the Head, from whom the whole body, supported and held together by its ligaments and sinews, grows as God causes it to grow.

> Since you died with Christ to the basic principles of this world, why, as though you still belonged to it, do you submit to its rules: "Do not handle! Do not taste! Do not touch!"? These are all destined to perish with use, because they are based on human commands and teachings. Such regulations indeed have an appearance of wisdom, with their self-imposed worship, their false humility and their harsh treatment of the body, but they lack any value in restraining sensual indulgence. (Colossians 2:16-23)

Our ultimate reality is found in Christ alone. He alone is our *Real* and *Lasting*. This is the reality of the Kingdom of God —*the way it really is.*

Why build on shadows and earthly reflections of rightness when we can embrace the one who is our righteousness? Whenever we turn from our trusting relationship with Jesus, we have fallen from the grace—the grace to live in the Kingdom and share in his righteousness. As Paul says, this is like a body losing connection to its head: oh, how absolutely awful to think of it. The result would be instant death. Why do we think the consequences in Christ's spiritual body would be any less severe? We should not make light of the horrible fate of giving ourselves over to the traditions of men instead of nurturing a simple, unwavering love for Christ alone. I can hear the passion of Paul's watchcare over our souls when he says to the believers in Galatia,

> You foolish Galatians! Who has bewitched you? Before your very eyes Jesus Christ was clearly portrayed as crucified. I would like to learn just one thing from you: Did you receive the Spirit by observing the law, or by believing what you heard? Are you so foolish? After

beginning with the Spirit, are you now trying to attain your goal by human effort? Have you suffered so much for nothing—if it really was for nothing? Does God give you his Spirit and work miracles among you because you observe the law, or because you believe what you heard? (Galatians 3:1-5)

We know that *the principles of this world* that Paul speaks of can affect people in many different ways. People of other eras and certainly in other religions have certainly tried to find their lives and meanings inside of these earthly principles. It is nothing new, and it is not in any way confined to Christian history. I have seen first-hand the principles of this world when I watched Russia deteriorate in the early nineties because of how Communism had shaped the grey hearts and faces of those people over generations. I have seen and smelled human tradition in central India as Hinduism and all of its earthly rituals and man-made beliefs diminished the worth of the individual and therefore the dark shape of society on the entire Indian sub-continent. I have also seen how the traditions of men have reduced the self-image and dreams of this present generation of Christian believers who struggle with who they are in God and who they are together as his people. Many of us really have been bewitched. It is as though the height of our organizational cathedrals—especially under the banner of great benevolent works—have, indeed, put us under a spell.

Breaking Free

Deliverance ministry anyone?

Seek first the Kingdom of God (Matthew 6:33).

This is the same vaccine we use to overcome our foolish obsessions with building the perfect Church and the subsequent diminishment of the very thing we thought we could perfect. We establish our main priority and never let it move.

Seek first the Kingdom of God.

This is where we learn who we are in God's eyes and what we share with Christ now that we live in him. This is the mind-freeing power of the Holy Spirit who convinces us of our place in God's heart as sons and frees us from weak imaginations. When we seek first the Kingdom, we never imagine ourselves able to be restricted by any man-made system.

Seek first the Kingdom of God.

This is how we learn the mental tools necessary to separate the traditions of men from the Church and from the Kingdom of God in healthy and helpful ways. This is how we discover the beauty of the Church and allow her to live free inside the Kingdom and never to be bound by any organization, large or small!

Seek first the Kingdom of God.

Put family first. Seeking the Kingdom is, first, the establishment of the family of God. Social engineering, redemptive creativity, community building, and helpful advocacy are not first. They are byproducts of the Kingdom of God, not the goal.

Seek first the Kingdom of God.

Worship what is worthy. Worship Christ alone. There is nothing and no one that deserves our affection more than Jesus. There is nothing more cleansing to our hearts than to abandon ourselves in thankful worship to God alone and set everything else down below him.

Seek first the Kingdom of God.

Make people the priority. If we really love people more than our projects—more than our systems—there is almost no way to fall under the spell of trusting in tradition. It is love for people that rules over the growling noise of pride, and it is love for people that purifies our use of the gifts God gave us, and it is love for people that focuses our life work into something eternally purposeful.

Seek first the Kingdom of God.

Avoid radicalism because it fails to lay hold of the Kingdom. It can protest what it doesn't like and it can offend anyone it doesn't agree with, but it is not the way of sons. The sons of God are destined for greatness, and being the opposition party is not intrinsically great. Proclaiming the Kingdom of God is intrinsically great. We establish the Kingdom now, wherever we go, whether it is perceived as radical or not because it is our joy simply to live in the favor of our Father and walk as his sons.

PART THREE:
MAKING IT PRACTICAL

In this the final section of this small book I want to be informal in my tone and direct in my approach to this question: How do we make these encouragements practical right now and apply them to our lives?

What follows are collections of activities, actions, and other practical steps towards becoming a Kingdom person. For myself, I call it "becoming a family man." Others might call it becoming a family woman, or a family leader, or a family pioneer, or a family member ... I like them all. I have written a statement for each one in the first person so they all will be comfortable in our mouths as we read them aloud, pray them, and make our declarations. In other words, I start each action with an "I" statement so we can personalize each one.

Try them all.

Do them all at once, or spread them out over time—all the time—like I do.

Repeat until the desired affect is achieved.

Practical Prayers

Praying really works. I prefer to pray aloud so my own ears can hear the truth coming out of my mouth. I repeat myself often when I pray for the same reason we sing songs over and over again. Repetition is convincing. I invite you to pray with me the following Kingdom prayers.

I want more of the Kingdom.

I grew up in an environment where the tradition of Church life was everything, and so I fell quickly into perceiving my value and future only from that viewpoint. Of course, I was learning some Kingdom values, and yes, the Kingdom was coming in my life from the very first moment I saw Jesus ... but I sensed there was more. Tradition whispered to me, "This is all you get," but I remained, and remain, unsatisfied with its offer.

I want more!

I want to pray as Jesus taught me. I want more of the Kingdom to come here on earth as it is in Heaven! As a result, I have decided to pray like this:

Jesus, in this situation, may your Kingdom come. Let your Kingdom come here in this place as it is in Heaven. May the power of the Kingdom come right now and destroy the works of the enemy. I want to see your Kingdom. There is not enough family happening here so Father I pray for more of your Kingdom to come! I want more.

I ask God to give me hunger.

Sometimes my heart grows tired and my vision dim. Sometimes I have little or no interest in the things of God.

I have found that it is perfectly acceptable to ask God—who gives me even the will to obey him—for more hunger for heavenly things.

So I pray, Dear God, give me a hunger for you. Help me hunger for your Kingdom. Give me a hunger for intimacy with Christ. I want a deep hunger for the Holy Spirit. I want to desire your purposes in my life. I am not afraid to ask. I love to say, "More, Lord, more of you!" when I pray because it will be much better than, "Less, Lord, less of you!"

I ask for the Spirit of Adoption.

Many ask, "Why do we pray for the Spirit of adoption when we are already saved ... haven't we already received it?" Of course we received it, but I am still challenged now to be filled with it, to walk in it. Romans 8 says with emphasis, "For you did not receive a spirit that makes you a slave again to fear, but you received the Spirit of sonship." Even in this one verse I can see that some, like myself, have battled fear in the arena of trusting in God's adopting love. This passage goes on and puts the work of the Spirit of adoption into the present tense: "And by him we cry, 'Abba, Father.' The Spirit himself testifies with our spirit that we are God's children."

The Spirit of adoption is the Holy Spirit.

The more I receive the Holy Spirit, the more the Spirit of adoption will be released in me!

My Father wants to have an ongoing relationship with me. He sent the Spirit to help me cry out, "Daddy, Father God!" not just one time, but always and for the rest of my life! And so I pray:

Father, I want more of the Spirit of adoption to be poured out on me. Just as I want more hugs and kisses from my natural family as an assurance of their affection, I receive the Spirit of adoption which stirs my heart up for you as a son.

I receive you, Holy Spirit of adoption!

I love you, Dad!

I pray for the sick and the demonized.

When Jesus proclaimed the Kingdom, the blind were healed, the sick mended, and people were set free from the bondage of satanic power. He went about "proclaiming the good news of the Kingdom, and curing every disease and every sickness" and in Matt. 12:28 he makes clear, "But if it is by the Spirit of God that I cast out demons, then the Kingdom of God has come to you."

He taught his disciples to do the same. In Mark 6 Jesus, "calling the Twelve to him, he sent them out two by two and gave them authority over evil spirits [...] They went out and preached that people should repent. They drove out many demons and anointed many sick people with oil and healed them."

I am his disciple, too. I expect to do the same.

The Kingdom is powerful, and it transforms the broken world all around me. Everywhere I go the Kingdom is going. The Kingdom of God is forcefully advancing as the dominate, ultimate Kingdom. So why would I be timid around the powers of darkness?

Jesus makes it very clear when he first tells Peter "I will build my Church, and the gates of Hades will not overcome it" that the Church is a sure thing—a strong thing. I know that when the Church agrees with the Kingdom its power is unmistakable. I agree with the Kingdom, and so I pray for the sick, asking God to heal them.

I cast out demons. I will discern the spirits of darkness and exercise my authority as a Kingdom son over them.

I demand that the suffering world around me submit to the authority of the Kingdom of God.

I pray for the unity of the family.

I do this in agreement with the Spirit of God and the prayers of Christ in John 17:

My prayer is not for them alone. I pray also for those who will believe in me through their message, that all of them may be one, Father, just as you are in me and I am in you. May they also be in us so that the world may believe that you have sent me. I have given them the glory that you gave me, that they may be one as we are one: I in them and you in me. May they be brought to complete unity to let the world know that you sent me and have loved them even as you have loved me.

I agree with Jesus.

This is our heart for one another in prayer.

Let it be.

Practical Receiving and Believing

Sometimes we need to take our hands off the hammers and saws, stop working, and just receive. When we are at rest and we pray about receiving the Kingdom, we sometimes just need to sit with our palms up and open as a physical expression of our hearts to God—just as if we were going to receive a gift from someone. We can imagine that our hands are still open, like our hearts are open, to the giver of all good gifts. It is good to receive his gifts and then to believe they are for us and good for us in every way.

I receive the Kingdom.

Jesus claimed the Church as something tangible that he could see with his eyes. I can claim her and see her, too.

The Kingdom, however, is different. It is a heavenly Kingdom. I need to exercise my faith in it. I choose to receive it by faith! Whenever I see the Kingdom reality around me I receive it. Whenever I understand a Kingdom value I adopt it into my heart. Whatever Jesus says about the family Kingdom I say, "Yes, Lord!" I encourage myself to not argue with the Kingdom.

When I read the parables of Jesus as he describes the Kingdom, I look for ways to receive and walk in the family truth they proclaim. These stories often begin with *the Kingdom of Heaven is like* or *the Kingdom of God can be compared to.* After I read them I say aloud, "This is the way the family works. I submit myself to the Kingdom."

I receive the baptism of the Holy Spirit.

Jesus, baptize me with the Holy Spirit!

I ask for it by name. I know it is a gift from the Father for me, and I know that it is good.

The disciples waited in Jerusalem for the Spirit to baptize them even though Jesus had already breathed on them and said, "Receive the Holy Spirit" in John 20. In the same way, my walk with Jesus is not a formula lined out on a flow chart. I do not fret over timelines. I am free to enjoy and engage Jesus as my Lord and friend at all times. Jesus wants to baptize me with the Holy Spirit. So I ask for it.

I expect to speak in tongues and see miracles. Why not? I am not a second-class Christian. Why would I, in a desire to be progressive and modern, throw out the very thing that gives me the power to love and to be an agent of change? The Holy Spirit is Christ's joy to give. I don't want to diminish his joy by refusing a gift because my tradition has set up electric fences around it. I can never say, "Oh ... the Holy Spirit ... I got my dose. I'm good. Don't need any more." That would be so unnatural for a Kingdom son. I just receive, and I pray like this:

I ask you Jesus to baptize me with the Holy Spirit. I will allow others to lay hands on me and pray for me to receive the Holy Spirit. I receive the Father's good gift that convinces me I am his to come into my life and to surround me, fill me, and equip me in every way to walk as a Kingdom son.

I receive leaders.

The leadership graces listed in Ephesians 4 are people. I am open to living and loving people who are sent to equip me, challenge me, and lead me into maturity in Christ.

I will not allow unforgiveness or judgement against leaders to steal my ability to receive the people that Jesus has sent to me as apostles, prophets, pastors and teachers, and evangelists. They are given to me to build me up in Christ.

Also, I will not get locked into only one leadership grace. If I only receive from one of Christ's graces for the Church then I will grow up abnormal and unfit for service, according to Ephesians 4. I have seen missionaries with hot, happening projects become debilitated after a while because they only had evangelist leaders. I have seen those who only received the leadership grace of the pastor-teacher, and they grew soft and immature in many areas. I have also seen those in prophetic camps sit still and grow satisfied with only seeing new visions, but they missed their time to labor and love and plant and work because their only leaders were prophets. No single grace-gift should ever be left alone in charge of God's people for long.

I will receive Christ who reveals himself differently in all of these leadership graces, and I will pray:

Father, I love leaders, please send me more.

I receive the apostles.

I receive the prophets.

I receive the pastors, the teachers, and the evangelists.

Practical Actions

Naming everything that Kingdom sons have the permission and ability to do is too long for a short book like this one. It is really not the stuff of books, either. It belongs in the space between family members who love one another and impart family values to one another. It is the stuff of fathers turning their hearts to their sons and the sons turning their hearts to their fathers. However, I have chosen to list a few basic Kingdom actions that will set us in a Kingdom direction.

I will continue to meet together with believers.

I will not let the enemy of my soul isolate me in some sort of personal spiritual journey track. Sons love to meet together for teaching and worship and prayer. I am a son.

In fact, Hebrews 10:25 makes it clear: "Let us not give up meeting together, as some are in the habit of doing, but let us encourage one another—and all the more as you see the Day approaching." So what if the last fellowship I went to offended me in some way? I was judging with human eyes and reasoning and now I need to forgive. I want to move on and obey God and connect with my family. I know that I can't fulfill God's dreams of family if I choose to walk alone, nor can I if I choose to sit lonely every Sunday in a room full of people I don't know. So here's how I pray:

Jesus, I want to be your friend. Help me make friends with your people. Help me to overcome past hurts. I will forgive them just as you have taught me. I will pursue deep Kingdom relationship with other believers and I will trust in no tradition to establish those relationships for me.

I will go where the good voices are helping me.

If every time my present leaders open their mouths they are diminishing others and dividing the family, then I will choose to stop listening to their teaching. I can still love them, but I can't follow immaturity. I will find another place to worship and fellowship.

I am not bound by tradition, but I am bound to seek and reconcile with healthy family. It isn't that hard to move—even across the country—and ultimately it is worth all the effort for the health of my own soul. I think I am agreeing with the spirit of Jesus' prayer in John 17: "I will remain in the world no longer, but they are still in the world, and I am coming to you. Holy Father, protect them by the power of your name—the name you gave me—so that they may be one as we are one." I want to be protected because I am worth protecting in the eyes of Jesus. Again, I choose:

Father, I receive your good gifts of good leaders. For the health of my soul give me the courage to move and connect with good people wherever they are so I can mature in your family.

I call out the names of the good leaders in my life and thank God for them on a regular basis. I send them gifts of thanksgiving and love. I serve them to show them I love them.

I will proclaim the Kingdom of God.

I am called to follow the model that Jesus set before me. I have received the Spirit of God that bubbles out of me in agreement. I will claim and love the Church as the Bride of Christ, and I will commit to proclaiming the arrival of the Kingdom of God.

To proclaim the Kingdom is to first announce that the King is here! He is not my teacher like Buddha. He is not my prophet like Mohammed. He is my King and his Kingdom knows no worthy adversary.

I let people know that the power of God is here to heal and that help is available now. I encourage them to repent from a self-led, self-promoting life and to turn to God.

I touch the sick and pray for their healing, I pray over the demon-possessed and they are set free, and I pray over the broken and they are put back together. Why? Because the Kingdom is advancing and I have no choice but to agree with it.

I don't work in my own authority but under the direction of my Father who has sent me as his son to do his heart's work. His heart is my heart. I am his son.

I will give generously without prejudice.

One of the ways that sons combat prejudice and division is through joyful giving. 2 Corinthians 9:7 tells us God loves a cheerful giver, and so I will cheerfully give toward love and connection in the family even more.

I will give to the Church of my city, not just the Church in a building.

I will give to those who watch over my soul first, but I also will give to those who faithfully lead others in order to encourage them and bless them. I will give to those in my spiritual family that I disagree with, just to give division no room to grow.

Anytime the devil tries to get me to shrink back from a Kingdom relationship I will give even more until he learns his lesson. Anytime the liar attacks me with fear of loss and bankruptcy, then I will give more just to make him look stupid.

I am writing a check right now.

I will claim the Church.

Jesus set a clear example for me in simply seeing and claiming the Church. I don't wish to claim it like I own it, as though it was an organization, but I do wish to lay claim to healthy relationships with the believers that I can see!

I will write down the names of believers around me that I can have a relationship with and claim them as my spiritual family. I am making that list right now.

I will call them Church.

For some I will parent, with some I will partner, and from some I will learn. I don't mind mixing that up a bit because our spiritual family life is fluid and intensely relational and is not set in static positions as some traditionalists like to pretend.

My Church of responsibility will be as big as my ability to receive them by name.

The Church in my imagination will go on to receive all of God's beautiful people around the whole world into my heart.

I will be a hero of reconciliation.

In 2 Corinthians 5 we know that "we regard no one from a worldly point of view," which is to say that we see according to the Spirit instead of the prejudices of the temporal world.

The passage continues: "Therefore, if anyone is in Christ, he is a new creation; the old has gone, the new has come!"

And just what is the result of this re-creation? "All this is from God, who reconciled us to himself through Christ and gave us the ministry of reconciliation."

I can be sure that I have been given one ministry that I am expected to become great at: the ministry of bringing people together! So I choose to say aloud:

God, help me become a great reconciler of people with you and of people together with one another. I am your ambassador of family love and healing forgiveness.

Practical Thinking

Here is a short review of the foundation stones for Kingdom thinking. I suggest writing them onto individual notecards and digesting each one over time. We could take some time to find our favorite Scripture for each one.

The Church and the Kingdom are not the same.

One is the people and one is the purpose. One is the body and one is the DNA code. One is finite, one is infinite. One is revealed in the earth; one is poured out from Heaven. I claim one, and I proclaim one. The Church has the choice to agree with the Kingdom in real time, but the Kingdom is a concrete, eternal reality that is unchanging in the heart of God.

I will choose my battles wisely.

I will not not war against people who are trapped in the traditions of men because this is wrong thinking. I love people. I may refuse their weak ideas, but I can still love them. I should feel free to reject being owned by any system that sets itself against the knowledge of Christ and the Kingdom of God, but why would I burn down buildings when there are good people inside? I am not an anti-tradition person; I am a pro-Kingdom person. The difference is important.

The way it really is.

When I come to a new situation or face a new problem I ask, "What is really happening here?" The first impression I get from my eyes and ears is not as important as what is really happening. It is the Kingdom view of a situation that is my reality.

My favorite everyday definition of the Kingdom of God is this: The Kingdom of God is *the way it really is.* The way everything meaningful and lasting and good really is—is the Kingdom.

It is time I simply begin to look for it and to agree with this heavenly reality everywhere I go. I am a son who belongs to a heavenly Kingdom, so I can act, at any time, in accordance with *the way it really is.* I don't have to act the way others expect me to act or the way others would see a situation and act. The Kingdom gives me new vision.

New ways of "doing Church" do not impress me.

There are many ways of meeting together as believers, and there are different structures and leadership styles. It is foolish to attach myself to only one with prejudice toward the rest.

Small, big, young, old, formal, casual, basic, or wild, the Church is always God's people. If they do things differently in different places, well ... so what?

I am interested in helping others mature in Christ. I hear and partner with Paul's heart for the Colossians:

> For this reason, since the day we heard about you, we have not stopped praying for you and asking God to fill you with the knowledge of his will through all spiritual wisdom and understanding. And we pray this in order that you may live a life worthy of the Lord and may please him in every way: bearing fruit in every good work, growing in the knowledge of God, being strengthened with all power according to his glorious might so that you may have great endurance and patience, and joyfully giving thanks to the Father, who has qualified you to share in the inheritance of the saints in the Kingdom of light. For he has rescued us from the dominion of darkness and brought us into the Kingdom of the Son he loves, in whom we have redemption, the forgiveness of sins [...] We proclaim him, admonishing and teaching everyone with all wisdom, so that we may present everyone perfect in Christ." (Colossians 1:9-14,28)

I don't war against those who are not like me.

I don't rage against other Christ-loving peoples.

I have stopped competing with other fellowships. I quit bashing the charismatics. I quit lampooning the quiet traditionalists. It was a waste of time, and it is just not what Kingdom sons do.

So what if that other bunch has done and taught some crazy things that I don't agree with? My traditional environment is far from perfect.

I have never met a family whose membership was built on agreement. Families are built on blood and adoption. I want to get my mind renewed with a vision for God's family. I will work out my own salvation with fear and trembling and not let judgement and prejudice stunt my growth or bring harm to his family.

I choose the Tree of Life.

There were two trees in the garden and I can still choose to eat from either one today. If I only want to eat from the Tree of the Knowledge of Good and Evil, then I will live and die inside of the judgements and divisions that I bring to everything, and frankly, no one will want to invite me to their parties.

When I choose to eat from the Tree of Life then Christ pours out on me the wine of joy and the oil of healing. I am a joy to be around. I can leave the old ways of measuring and striving and fear behind.

I find that choosing to worship God with abandon helps me eat from the Tree of Life. I can say goodbye to all judgements and focus on the beautiful face of Jesus and worship him!

Practical Tradition Tester

Everywhere I go I meet two distinct kinds of people: those who want the life of the Kingdom and those who don't. Some really want to see the Kingdom come more and they welcome the revolution. There are others, however, who just want to defend what they have known according to their traditions. Here are questions that will help us discern ourselves.

Do I refer to a building as the Church?

I repent for using the beautiful word Church to identify a building. I won't do it any more. I will use the word Church only for the people of God.

Do I say, "I am going to Church."?

Well, of course, this is craziness. It is like saying, "I am going to family" when we get off work and start the drive home. So, I repent for ever "going to Church" and I won't do it any more.

Do I use possessive words in reference to Church?

The words "mine," "yours," and "theirs" are possessive pronouns. The Church is neither mine nor yours. It is neither theirs nor ours. The Church belongs to no man because it belongs completely to Jesus. We belong to it.

I repent.

Do I love to be mentored or do I shy from leadership?

I repent, God, and I ask you to show me the root of my rebellion. Is it wounding? Is it pride? Is it hiding from the light?

Is it just poor training in my youth? Whatever it is, I am willing to face it and see myself healed so I can receive good leadership.

Am I more obsessed with projects or with people?

I repent for ever serving projects before I would serve people. I pray that people would grow larger and larger in my imagination and more beautiful to me every day so that I can have your eyes, Jesus. I want to be the person who shuts down projects when people are hurting, never the other way around.

Do I struggle with understanding the Kingdom?

I confess that I am a product of my tradition, and I have a weak mind. I need help. Help me, Jesus, to embrace the Kingdom message and the Kingdom truth so that I can both love the Church and proclaim your Kingdom.

Do I fence in the Holy Spirit so others will be safe?

Dear Holy Spirit, I want to be your friend. I do not want to treat you like an unruly child—or a untrustworthy adult—anymore. You are beautiful, necessary, trustworthy, and you are God. I release you in my life and in the world around me to be yourself.

Practical Meditations

Meditation in its simplest form is an idea worth repeating. Here are some ideas worth repeating. We can repeat them to ourselves. We can write them in our journals and put them in our songs. Let's find a quiet place, close the door, and repeat these beautiful meditations aloud.

I am my Father's favorite son.

Yes, I am my Father's favorite son. We are all his favorites! This is the way Dad loves us. He loves us so much that we are each his favorites. I am his dearly beloved and I will be carefully taken care of. I have no fear about his preserving love ever losing its power or affection for me.

I am in agreement with God.

I am an instrument that makes a beautiful sound, and my most beautiful sound is the one that harmonizes with the heart of God. The Kingdom is like a song and I am carefully listening so I can join in. Since I have been reborn into the Kingdom of God, this song is so natural for me. It sounds like home. I am coming home. I live in harmony with God as Christ surrounds me. I agree with God.

The Holy Spirit is full-on.

The Kingdom of God is here when Christ appears, and now, by the Holy Spirit, he appears in us! The Kingdom advances as we, the sons of God, continue to receive it and proclaim it. The coming of the Kingdom is a fluid, present reality and the sons of God are authorized to act in accordance with it. I am a

Kingdom agent. I can release what is in Heaven right here on the earth! I have abandoned the misinformed teachings on how gifts, miracles, and graces died with the apostles of the Lamb in the first century A.D. Most have done this to excuse their own lack of power, but not us—we are empowered sons and a people of faith! We are full of the power of the Holy Spirit.

I expect the miracle of salvation all around me.

We call out to the lost and invite them to join us in the heavenly family, not just to join us at a Church meeting. We invite others to repent and believe in Jesus, be reunited with Father, and enter the Kingdom of God. They will become part of the Church as a relational byproduct. We believe for all to receive the baptism of the Holy Spirit as the obvious gift of God to empower us to live according to the Kingdom's expectations, just as the apostles in th e New Testament expected it for anyone who chose to repent and follow Jesus. Salvation is available for everyone around me.

I am ready for rejection, but it does not define me.

Jesus quotes the mission statement of the Kingdom in Isaiah 61 when he first speaks publicly in a religious meeting. He was in his hometown of Nazareth, in Luke 4, and the meeting did not end well. In fact, it ended in religious folks trying to throw him off of a cliff. As soon as I begin to proclaim the Kingdom some will be immediately ready to throw me off a cliff, too. If I teach Kingdom responsibility some will receive it as an offense. Some will see it as the giving of a new law or a new way for people to fail. This reaction is common, even among good people, when believers have learned to love and protect their form of Church more than they understand proclaiming the Kingdom.

I will not judge those who do not hear. I receive my charge to equip the saints and encourage the family, even the judgmental members of the family. I am going to take up my personal responsibility, and I am going to mature in Christ.

I will not glory in being rejected. My glory will be my love for the family of God.

I am like my Dad.

I am like my Dad. It is natural for me to obey him, and it is unnatural for me to disagree with him. I am a son who is destined to become like his Father, and I will show my transformation by saying that I believe that *I am a son now* through my faith in Christ alone. I will receive the Kingdom and enjoy my favored position in the eyes of my Father. I am beginning to shine as it says I will in Matthew 13:43:

"Then the righteous will shine like the sun in the Kingdom of their Father."

BIBLE-OGRAPHY

The Kingdom as a *Way*

The good news of the Kingdom is preached, people are healed, baptized, and the end is prophesied.

Matt. 4:23 Jesus went throughout Galilee, teaching in their synagogues, preaching the good news of the Kingdom, and healing every disease and sickness among the people.

Matt. 9:35 Jesus went through all the towns and villages, teaching in their synagogues, preaching the good news of the Kingdom and healing every disease and sickness.

Luke 4:43 But he said, "I must preach the good news of the Kingdom of God to the other towns also, because that is why I was sent."

Luke 8:1 After this, Jesus traveled about from one town and village to another, proclaiming the good news of the Kingdom of God. The Twelve were with him,

Luke 16:16 The Law and the Prophets were proclaimed until John. Since that time, the good news of the Kingdom of God is being preached, and everyone is forcing his way into it.

Matt. 24:14 And this gospel of the Kingdom will be preached in the whole world as a testimony to all nations, and then the end will come.

Luke 9:2 and he sent them out to preach the Kingdom of God and to heal the sick.

Luke 9:11 but the crowds learned about it and followed him. He welcomed them and spoke to them about the Kingdom of God, and healed those who needed healing.

Acts 1:3 After his suffering, he showed himself to these men and gave many convincing proofs that he was alive. He appeared to them over a period of forty days and spoke about the Kingdom of God.

Acts 8:12 But when they believed Philip as he preached the good news of the Kingdom of God and the name of Jesus Christ, they were baptized, both men and women.

Acts 19:8 Paul entered the synagogue and spoke boldly there for three months, arguing persuasively about the Kingdom of God.

Acts 28:23 They arranged to meet Paul on a certain day, and came in even larger numbers to the place where he was staying. From morning till evening he explained and declared to them the Kingdom of God and tried to convince them about Jesus from the Law of Moses and from the Prophets.

Acts 28:31 Boldly and without hindrance he preached the Kingdom of God and taught about the Lord Jesus Christ.

Acts 20:25 Now I know that none of you among whom I have gone about preaching the Kingdom will ever see me again.

The Kingdom can be inherited by some, and given to others

Luke 18:16 But Jesus called the children to him and said, "Let the little children come to me, and do not hinder them, for the Kingdom of God belongs to such as these."

Matt. 5:3 Blessed are the poor in spirit, for theirs is the Kingdom of Heaven.

Matt. 5:10 Blessed are those who are persecuted because of righteousness, for theirs is the Kingdom of Heaven.

Luke 6:20 Looking at his disciples, he said: "Blessed are you who are poor, for yours is the Kingdom of God.

Matt. 25:34 Then the King will say to those on his right, "Come, you who are blessed by my Father; take your inheritance, the Kingdom prepared for you since the creation of the world."

Parable of the Wedding Party: Matt. 22:8 Then he said to his servants, "The wedding banquet is ready, but those I invited did not deserve to come. Go to the street corners and invite to the banquet anyone you find." So the servants went out into the streets and gathered all the people they could find, both good and bad, and the wedding hall was filled with guests.

Parable of the Five Wise Virgins: Matt. 25:10 But while they were on their way to buy the oil, the Bridegroom arrived. The virgins who were ready went in with him to the wedding banquet. And the door was shut.

Parable of the Responsible Servants: Matt. 25:28-29a Take the talent from him and give it to the one who has the ten talents. For everyone who has will be given more, and he will have an abundance.

The Parable of the Sheep and the Goats: Matt. 25:34-36 Then the King will say to those on his right, "Come, you who are blessed by my Father; take your inheritance, the Kingdom prepared for you since the creation of the world. For I was hungry and you gave me something to eat, I was thirsty and you gave me something to drink, I was a stranger and you invited me in, I needed clothes and you clothed me, I was sick and you looked after me, I was in prison and you came to visit me."

Parable of the Wheat and Weeds: Matt. 13:37-39, 43 He answered, "The one who sowed the good seed is the Son of Man. The field is the world, and the good seed stands for the sons of the kingdom. The weeds are the sons of the evil one, and the enemy who sows them is the devil. The harvest is the end of the age, and the harvesters are angels [who throw the weeds away] [...] Then the righteous will shine like the sun in the Kingdom of their Father. He who has ears, let him hear.

Parable of the Sower: Matt. 13:18, 23 Listen then to what the parable of the sower means: [many seeds don't grow] [...] But the one who received the seed that fell on good soil is the man who hears the word and understands it. He produces a crop, yielding a hundred, sixty or thirty times what was sown.

Some will not inherit the Kingdom

Matt. 13:41 The Son of Man will send out his angels, and they will weed out of his Kingdom everything that causes sin and all who do evil.

Parable of the Wedding Party: Matt. 22:5-7, 11-13 But they paid no attention and went off—one to his field, another to his business. The rest seized his servants, mistreated them and killed them. The king was enraged. He sent his army and destroyed those murderers and burned their city [...] But when the king came in to see the guests, he noticed a man there who was not wearing wedding clothes. "Friend," he asked, "how did you get in here without wedding clothes?" The man was speechless. Then the king told the attendants, "Tie him hand and foot, and throw him outside, into the darkness, where there will be weeping and gnashing of teeth."

Parable of the Five Wise Virgins: Matt. 25:11-12 Later the others also came. "Sir! Sir!" they said. "Open the door for us!" But he replied, "I tell you the truth, I don't know you."

Parable of the Responsible Servants: Matt.25:29b-30 Whoever does not have, even what he has will be taken from him [...] And throw that worthless servant outside, into the darkness, where there will be weeping and gnashing of teeth.

The Parable of the Sheep and the Goats: Matt. 25:44-46 They also will answer, 'Lord, when did we see you hungry or thirsty or a stranger or needing clothes or sick or in prison, and did not help you?" He will reply, 'I tell you the truth, whatever you did not do for one of the least of these, you did not do for me.' Then they will go away to eternal punishment, but the righteous to eternal life.

Parable of the Fishing Net: Matt. 13:47-50 Once again, the Kingdom of Heaven is like a net that was let down into the lake and caught all kinds of fish [...] When it was full, the fishermen pulled it up on the shore. Then they sat down and collected the good fish in baskets, but threw the bad away. This is how it will be at the end of the age. The angels will come and separate the wicked from the righteous and throw them into the fiery furnace, where there will be weeping and gnashing of teeth.

Parable of the Wheat and Weeds: Matt. 13:37-42 He answered, "The one who sowed the good seed is the Son of Man. The field is the world, and the good seed stands for the sons of the Kingdom. The weeds are the sons of the evil one, and the enemy who sows them is the devil. The harvest is the end of the age, and the harvesters are angels. As the weeds are pulled up and burned in the fire, so it will be at the end of the age. The Son of Man will send out his angels, and they will weed out of his Kingdom everything that causes sin and all who do evil. They will throw them into the fiery furnace, where there will be weeping and gnashing of teeth."

Parable of the Sower: Matt. 13:18-22 Listen then to what the parable of the sower means: "When anyone hears the message about the Kingdom and does not understand it, the evil one comes and snatches away what was sown in his heart. This is the seed sown along the path. The one who received the seed that fell on rocky places is the man who hears the word and at once receives it with joy. But since he has no root, he lasts only a short time. When trouble or persecution comes because of the word, he quickly falls away. The one who received the seed that fell among the thorns is the man who hears the word, but the worries of this life and the deceitfulness of wealth choke it, making it unfruitful."

Acts 1:6 So when they met together, they asked him, "Lord, are you at this time going to restore the Kingdom to Israel?"

1 Cor. 6:9-10 Do you not know that the wicked will not inherit the Kingdom of God? Do not be deceived: Neither the sexually immoral nor idolaters nor adulterers nor male prostitutes nor homosexual offenders nor thieves nor the greedy nor drunkards nor slanderers nor swindlers will inherit the Kingdom of God.

1 Cor. 15:50 I declare to you, brothers, that flesh and blood cannot inherit the Kingdom of God, nor does the perishable inherit the imperishable.

Gal. 5:19-21 The acts of the sinful nature are obvious: sexual immorality, impurity and debauchery; idolatry and witchcraft; hatred, discord, jealousy, fits of rage, selfish ambition, dissensions, factions and envy; drunkenness, orgies, and the like. I warn you, as I did before, that those who live like this will not inherit the Kingdom of God.

Col. 1:12-13 [Give] thanks to the Father, who has qualified you to share in the inheritance of the saints in the Kingdom of light. For he has rescued us from the dominion of darkness and brought us into the Kingdom of the Son he loves.

The Kingdom can be pursued and obtained

Matt. 11:11-12 I tell you the truth: Among those born of women there has not risen anyone greater than John the Baptist; yet he who is least in the Kingdom of Heaven is greater than he. From the days of John the Baptist until now, the Kingdom of Heaven has been forcefully advancing, and forceful men lay hold of it.

Matt. 6:33 But seek first his Kingdom and his righteousness, and all these things will be given to you as well.

Luke 12:31 But seek his Kingdom, and these things will be given to you as well.

Parable of the Treasure in a Field: Matt. 13:44 The Kingdom of Heaven is like treasure hidden in a field. When a man found it, he hid it again, and then in his joy went and sold all he had and bought that field.

Parable of the Fine Pearl: Matt. 13:45-46 Again, the Kingdom of Heaven is like a merchant looking for fine pearls. When he found one of great value, he went away and sold everything he had and bought it.

The Kingdom is powerful and growing
and it transforms all it touches

Parable of the Yeast and Bread: Matt. 13:33-35 He told them still another parable: "The Kingdom of Heaven is like yeast that a woman took and mixed into a large amount of flour until it worked all through the dough." Jesus spoke all these things to the crowd in parables; he did not say anything to them without using a parable. So was fulfilled what was spoken through the prophet: "I will open my mouth in parables, I will utter things hidden since the creation of the world."

Parable of the Tiny Seed: Matt. 13:31-32 He told them another parable: "The Kingdom of Heaven is like a mustard seed, which a man took and planted in his field. Though it is the smallest of all your seeds, yet when it grows, it is the largest of garden plants and becomes a tree, so that the birds of the air come and perch in its branches."

Matt. 16:19 I will give you the keys of the Kingdom of Heaven; whatever you bind on earth will be bound in Heaven, and whatever you loose on earth will be loosed in Heaven.

The Kingdom of God is a way of spiritual living

Luke 9:62 Jesus replied, "No one who puts his hand to the plow and looks back is fit for service in the Kingdom of God."

Matt. 19:12 For some are eunuchs because they were born that way; others were made that way by men; and others have renounced marriage because of the Kingdom of Heaven. The one who can accept this should accept it.

Parable of the Responsible Servants: Matt. 25:14-17 Again, it will be like a man going on a journey, who called his servants and entrusted his property to them. To one he gave five talents of money, to another two talents, and to another one talent, each according to his ability. Then he went on his journey. The man who had received the five talents went at once and put his money to work and gained five more. So also, the one with the two talents gained two more.

Parable of the Sheep and the Goats: Matt. 25:34-40 Then the King will say to those on his right, "Come, you who are blessed by my Father; take your inheritance, the Kingdom prepared for you since the creation of the world. For I was hungry and you gave me something to eat, I was thirsty and you gave me something to drink, I was a stranger and you invited me in, I needed clothes and you clothed me, I was sick and you looked after me, I was in prison and you came to visit me." Then the righteous will answer him, "Lord, when did we see you hungry and feed you, or thirsty and give you something to drink? When did we see you a stranger and invite you in, or needing clothes and clothe you? When did we see you sick or in prison and go to visit you?" The King will reply, "I tell you the truth, whatever you did for one of the least of these brothers of mine, you did for me."

Parable of the Unforgiving Servant: Matt. 18:32-35 Then the master called the servant in. "You wicked servant," he said, "I canceled all that debt of yours because you begged me to. Shouldn't you have had mercy on your fellow servant just as I had on you?" In anger his master turned him over to the jailers to be tortured, until he should pay back all he owed. This is how my heavenly Father will treat each of you unless you forgive your brother from your heart.

Mark 4:21-23 He said to them, "Do you bring in a lamp to put it under a bowl or a bed? Instead, don't you put it on its stand? For whatever is hidden is meant to be disclosed, and whatever is concealed is meant to be brought out into the open. If anyone has ears to hear, let him hear."

Mark 4:24-25 "Consider carefully what you hear," he continued. "With the measure you use, it will be measured to you —and even more. Whoever has will be given more; whoever does not have, even what he has will be taken from him."

Rom. 14:17 For the Kingdom of God is not a matter of eating and drinking, but of righteousness, peace and joy in the Holy Spirit,

1 Cor. 4:20 For the Kingdom of God is not a matter of talk but of power.

Col. 4:11 Jesus, who is called Justus, also sends greetings. These are the only Jews among my fellow workers for the Kingdom of God, and they have proved a comfort to me.

2 Thess. 1:5 All this is evidence that God's judgment is right, and as a result you will be counted worthy of the Kingdom of God, for which you are suffering.

There is a relational structure in the Kingdom

Luke 7:28 I tell you, among those born of women there is no one greater than John; yet the one who is least in the Kingdom of God is greater than he.

Luke 9:60 Jesus said to him, "Let the dead bury their own dead, but you go and proclaim the Kingdom of God."

Matt. 18:1-4 At that time the disciples came to Jesus and asked, "Who is the greatest in the Kingdom of Heaven?" He called a little child and had him stand among them. And he said, "I tell you the truth, unless you change and become like little children, you will never enter the Kingdom of Heaven. Therefore, whoever humbles himself like this child is the greatest in the Kingdom of Heaven."

Parable of the Last Minute Hiring: Matt. 20:13-16 But he answered one of them, "Friend, I am not being unfair to you. Didn't you agree to work for a denarius? Take your pay and go. I want to give the man who was hired last the same as I gave you. Don't I have the right to do what I want with my own money? Or are you envious because I am generous?" So the last will be first, and the first will be last.

The Kingdom as a *Place*

Requirements for entering the Kingdom

John 3:3 In reply, Jesus declared, "I tell you the truth, no one can see the Kingdom of God unless he is born again."

John 3:5 Jesus answered, "I tell you the truth, no one can enter the Kingdom of God unless he is born of water and the Spirit.

Matt. 5:20 For I tell you that unless your righteousness surpasses that of the Pharisees and the teachers of the law, you will certainly not enter the Kingdom of Heaven.

Matt. 7:21 Not everyone who says to me, "Lord, Lord," will enter the Kingdom of Heaven, but only he who does the will of my Father who is in Heaven.

Entering the Kingdom is sometimes hard

Luke 16:16 The Law and the Prophets were proclaimed until John. Since that time, the good news of the Kingdom of God is being preached, and everyone is forcing his way into it.

Mark 9:47 And if your eye causes you to sin, pluck it out. It is better for you to enter the Kingdom of God with one eye than to have two eyes and be thrown into hell.

Mark 10:24-25 The disciples were amazed at his words. But Jesus said again, "Children, how hard it is to enter the Kingdom of God! It is easier for a camel to go through the eye of a needle than for a rich man to enter the Kingdom of God."

Matt. 23:13 Woe to you, teachers of the law and Pharisees, you hypocrites! You shut the Kingdom of Heaven in men's faces. You yourselves do not enter, nor will you let those enter who are trying to.

Matt. 21:31 "Which of the two did what his father wanted?" "The first," they answered. Jesus said to them, "I tell you the truth, the tax collectors and the prostitutes are entering the Kingdom of God ahead of you."

Acts 14:22 "We must go through many hardships to enter the Kingdom of God," they said.

Entering the Kingdom is sometimes easy

Matt. 18:3-4 And he said: "I tell you the truth, unless you change and become like little children, you will never enter the Kingdom of Heaven. Therefore, whoever humbles himself like this child is the greatest in the Kingdom of Heaven."

2 Tim. 4:18 The Lord will rescue me from every evil attack and will bring me safely to his heavenly Kingdom. To him be glory for ever and ever. Amen.

2 Pet. 1:11 and you will receive a rich welcome into the eternal Kingdom of our Lord and Savior Jesus Christ

The Kingdom can come to us,
and it can be given to us

Matt. 12:28 But if I drive out demons by the Spirit of God, then the Kingdom of God has come upon you.

Luke 11:2 He said to them, "When you pray, say: 'Father, hallowed be your name, your Kingdom come.'

Luke 22:29-30 And I confer on you a kingdom, just as my Father conferred one on me, so that you may eat and drink at my table in my Kingdom and sit on thrones, judging the twelve tribes of Israel.

Luke 11:20 But if I drive out demons by the finger of God, then the Kingdom of God has come to you.

Matt. 21:43 Therefore I tell you that the Kingdom of God will be taken away from you and given to a people who will produce its fruit.

Mark 4:11 He told them, "The secret of the Kingdom of God has been given to you. But to those on the outside everything is said in parables."

Luke 12:32 Do not be afraid, little flock, for your Father has been pleased to give you the Kingdom.

The Kingdom is a nearby place or entity

Mark 1:15 "The time has come," he said. "The Kingdom of God is near. Repent and believe the good news!"

Mark 12:34 When Jesus saw that he had answered wisely, he said to him, "You are not far from the Kingdom of God." And from then on no one dared ask him any more questions.

Luke 10:11 Even the dust of your town that sticks to our feet we wipe off against you. Yet be sure of this: The Kingdom of God is near.

Luke 10:9 Heal the sick who are there and tell them, "The Kingdom of God is near you."

Luke 21:31 Even so, when you see these things happening, you know that the Kingdom of God is near.

Matt. 3:2 Repent, for the Kingdom of Heaven is near.

Matt. 4:17 From that time on Jesus began to preach, "Repent, for the Kingdom of Heaven is near."

Matt. 10:7 As you go, preach this message: "The Kingdom of Heaven is near."

John 18:36 Jesus said, "My Kingdom is not of this world. If it were, my servants would fight to prevent my arrest by the Jews. But now my Kingdom is from another place."

The Kingdom will be relevant in the future

Mark 9:1 And he said to them, "I tell you the truth, some who are standing here will not taste death before they see the Kingdom of God come with power."

Mark 14:25 I tell you the truth, I will not drink again of the fruit of the vine until that day when I drink it anew in the Kingdom of God.

Mark 15:43 Joseph of Arimathea, a prominent member of the Council, who was himself waiting for the Kingdom of God, went boldly to Pilate and asked for Jesus' body.

Luke 9:27 I tell you the truth, some who are standing here will not taste death before they see the Kingdom of God.

Luke 19:11 While they were listening to this, he went on to tell them a parable, because he was near Jerusalem and the people thought that the Kingdom of God was going to appear at once.

Matt. 13:43 Then the righteous will shine like the sun in the Kingdom of their Father. He who has ears, let him hear.

Luke 22:16 For I tell you, I will not eat it again until it finds fulfillment in the Kingdom of God.

Luke 22:18 For I tell you I will not drink again of the fruit of the vine until the Kingdom of God comes.

Matt. 8:11 I say to you that many will come from the east and the west, and will take their places at the feast with Abraham, Isaac and Jacob in the Kingdom of Heaven.

Matt. 16:28 I tell you the truth, some who are standing here will not taste death before they see the Son of Man coming in his Kingdom.

Luke 13:28-29 There will be weeping there, and gnashing of teeth, when you see Abraham, Isaac and Jacob and all the prophets in the Kingdom of God, but you yourselves thrown out. People will come from east and west and north and south, and will take their places at the feast in the Kingdom of God.

Luke 14:15 When one of those at the table with him heard this, he said to Jesus, "Blessed is the man who will eat at the feast in the Kingdom of God."

Matt. 26:29 I tell you, I will not drink of this fruit of the vine from now on until that day when I drink it anew with you in my Father's Kingdom.

The Kingdom is within us

Luke 17:20-21 Once, having been asked by the Pharisees when the Kingdom of God would come, Jesus replied, "The Kingdom of God does not come with your careful observation, nor will people say, 'Here it is,' or 'There it is,' because the Kingdom of God is within you."

www.benpasley.com

LaVergne, TN USA
24 November 2009
165050LV00004B/5/P